The Spanish Conquest of the Americas

An Enthralling Overview of the Conquistadors and Their Conquests of the Aztec and Inca Empires

© Copyright 2023 - All rights reserved.

The content contained within this book may not be reproduced, duplicated, or transmitted without direct written permission from the author or the publisher.

Under no circumstances will any blame or legal responsibility be held against the publisher, or author, for any damages, reparation, or monetary loss due to the information contained within this book, either directly or indirectly.

Legal Notice:

This book is copyright protected. It is only for personal use. You cannot amend, distribute, sell, use, quote, or paraphrase any part, or the content within this book, without the consent of the author or publisher.

Disclaimer Notice:

Please note the information contained within this document is for educational and entertainment purposes only. All effort has been executed to present accurate, up-to-date, reliable, and complete information. No warranties of any kind are declared or implied. Readers acknowledge that the author is not engaging in the rendering of legal, financial, medical, or professional advice. The content within this book has been derived from various sources. Please consult a licensed professional before attempting any techniques outlined in this book.

By reading this document, the reader agrees that under no circumstances is the author responsible for any losses, direct or indirect, that are incurred as a result of the use of the information contained within this document, including, but not limited to, errors, omissions, or inaccuracies.

Free limited time bonus

Stop for a moment. We have a free bonus set up for you. The problem is this: we forget 90% of everything that we read after 7 days. Crazy fact, right? Here's the solution: we've created a printable, 1-page pdf summary for this book that you're reading now. All you have to do to get your free pdf summary is to go to the following website:

https://livetolearn.lpages.co/enthrallinghistory/

Once you do, it will be intuitive. Enjoy, and thank you!

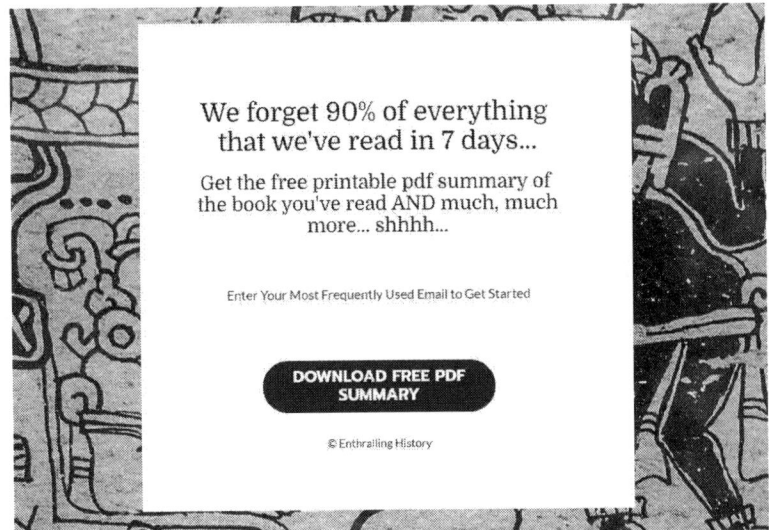

Table of Contents

INTRODUCTION 1
CHAPTER ONE - THE DISCOVERY OF AMERICA 4
CHAPTER TWO - EARLY CONQUISTADOR EXPEDITIONS 16
CHAPTER THREE - THE CONQUEST OF THE AZTEC EMPIRE................24
CHAPTER FOUR - SPAIN IN MESOAMERICA 50
CHAPTER FIVE - CONQUISTADORS IN SOUTH AMERICA 71
CHAPTER SIX - THE SPANISH CONQUEST OF THE INCA 82
CHAPTER SEVEN - SPANISH AMERICA 101
CONCLUSION..114
HERE'S ANOTHER BOOK BY ENTHRALLING HISTORY THAT YOU MIGHT LIKE..116
FREE LIMITED TIME BONUS...117
SOURCES..118

Introduction

There have not been many occurrences in the history of civilization that changed our perception of the world as much as the discovery of the Americas by Christopher Columbus in the late 15th century. As you might already know, a Viking named Leif Erikson had already discovered North America about five hundred years prior to Columbus's discovery. However, that knowledge was lost, and the rest of Europe was unaware of his discovery, making Columbus's discovery one of the most amazing developments of the medieval era. The story of Columbus and his expeditions is compelling from beginning to end, and its consequences cannot be overstated. The remarkable, albeit accidental, event caused a fundamental paradigm to shift and managed to change the way humans perceived the world.

Still, although the discovery of a whole new landmass brought Columbus fame and stamped his name in the history books forever, what is relatively unknown is the immediate history following this magnificent development. Indeed, Columbus was one of the spearheads of the Age of Exploration—a time when European nations were subsumed by the desire to find out more about the world in which they lived. They undertook daring ventures for practical and symbolic purposes. Great explorers like Columbus, Ferdinand Magellan, Vasco da Gama, and others managed to change our conception of the physical world and furthered the people's desire to explore. However, they also ushered in a new age of conquest and colonization.

The Europeans diverted a lot of their attention to aggressive expansion in the newly discovered lands, motivated partially by curiosity but mostly by material gains on a never-before-seen scale. The centuries following Columbus's expeditions are filled with struggles between the dwellers of the Old World and those living in the New World and the eventual costly victory of the former over the latter. Unlike Columbus's famous story, the conquest of the Americas is not necessarily a topic of detailed interest for those who cherish the explorer, but the story is instrumental, as it shaped people's understanding of the world.

This book will be focused on one aspect of the bigger story: the Spanish conquest of the Americas. Many nations tried their hand at colonizing and exploring the unknown, with some failing and others succeeding. However, perhaps no nation focused more on conquering the domains of the Americas than Spain. The resources and the overall effort diverted to Spanish colonial matters were immense, and in a way, they paid off. Spain managed to elevate its position from a relatively newly created nation that struggled to consolidate its power regionally to an empire that controlled a huge part of the known world.

Since the Spanish were one of the first to sail on these daring ventures of colonization, they managed to assert their technological dominance over the less-developed peoples of the Americas. They conquered lands and overwhelmed any opposition the natives put up. With the riches acquired in the New World, Spain quickly transformed into a superpower, maintaining its hold on its vast conquests for centuries before domestic and foreign troubles made the nation gradually withdraw from the Americas. Still, Spain left its mark on the two continents, influencing much of its sociocultural makeup, which we can still see today.

Of course, this book will only look at how Spain conquered the Americas; we will not delve too deep into the centuries of governance of the region and the social and political processes that developed. The opening chapters of the book will focus on the discovery of America by Christopher Columbus, recounting the story of the world-famous exploration and the struggles of the explorers. We will cover the general reception of this monumental development in Europe and the political and economic implications it had on Spain and its rival Portugal. After the discovery of the Americas, the Age of Exploration really kicked off, motivating many to go on daring naval and land ventures to find out more about the world.

The middle part of the book will talk about the arrival of the first Spanish conquistadors. They had one goal: to claim lands and riches in the name of Spain. Conquistadors were led by figures like Hernán Cortés and Pedro de Alvarado. They managed to defeat the native populations, conquering long-standing civilizations like the Aztecs and the Inca. We shall cover the conquistadors' expeditions to various parts of the Americas, first in Central America and the islands of the Caribbean, then their conquest of the Yucatán Peninsula, and finally, South America. The Spanish left their mark in all of these territories, which they acquired mostly through war.

Finally, the concluding chapters of the book will be concerned with the last major conquistador expeditions in the Americas in the late 16th century. We will look at the state of the known world about one hundred years after Columbus's initial discovery and assess the impact of the early Age of Exploration. Then, we will explore Spain's efforts to try and maintain a permanent presence in its colonies. It is interesting to look at the cultural influences the Spanish had on the natives and vice versa and how the relationship between the two developed. In the conclusion, we will talk about the immediate and long-lasting effects that the Spanish conquest of the Americas had on the world.

We hope you enjoy the book!

Chapter One – The Discovery of America

The Need to Explore

Europe was not at its best in the mid-15th century. The continent faced squabbles between its Catholic nations, all of which were weakened due to the constant wars with each other. In central Europe, the ever-so-unstable Holy Roman Empire was struggling for dominance with the papacy, an institution that was slowly losing its influence. France and England were also constantly at war with each other, while the Iberian Christians in Spain and Portugal were just finishing the centuries-long Reconquista against the Muslims. Most importantly, however, the power of Europe was undermined by the new superpowers in the east, namely the Muslim Ottoman Empire, which managed to destroy the final remnants of the once-great Byzantine Empire in 1453 when it captured Constantinople—one of the largest and richest cities at that time.

The recent rise of the Ottomans at the expense of the Christian Byzantines came at a great cost to Europe. The Ottoman Empire emerged from Anatolia, conquering the neighboring provinces one by one and consolidating its position along the former borders of the Byzantine Empire. It controlled territories in the Balkans, the Levant, Egypt, and North Africa. Due to the Ottomans' religious differences, they were perceived as a naturally hostile threat by the Europeans, but no kingdom was strong enough to directly challenge its might on the field of battle. The sheer vastness of the Ottomans and the relative weakening of the Europeans meant that the latter had to coexist with their new neighbors in the east and hope that they would not try to expand further in mainland Europe.

Perhaps the biggest problem with a strong Ottoman Empire was the fact that it basically controlled the main connecting trade routes between Europe and Asia. For centuries, the Christian Byzantine Empire had provided a corridor of trade with Persia and the Far East, with caravans traveling through Byzantine lands, their valuable goods eventually ending up in Europe. Asia provided Europe with luxurious materials and rare foods like spices, which the Europeans valued and massively depended upon. Trade also flowed through the Indian Ocean up the Red Sea to Egypt and from there through the Mediterranean Sea to the European continent.

However, especially after the fall of Constantinople, the Ottomans held a firm grip over the trade routes between the two continents. The Ottomans were hostile to most of the Christian nations, especially the biggest naval power of the Mediterranean and one of their long-standing rivals, Venice. The Ottomans basically monopolized the existing trade and made it far more difficult and expensive for Europeans to access the rich Asian markets. It soon became clear that going through the Ottoman lands was not the best option, so Europe had to find an alternative way to get to Asia.

So, the Europeans began to find a new way to Asia. One problem was that the seas outside of the Mediterranean were still largely unknown to the Europeans at that time, although some daring expeditions had already tried to journey to the west or south of the Atlantic, albeit to mixed success. Genoese merchants had sailed to the western coast of Africa, reaching the Azores and Madeira, but they did not achieve much beyond that, as they did not know what the ocean had in store for them. Still, the advancements in seafaring and cartography motivated many to overcome the challenging circumstances of the time.

One of the pioneers was Portugal's Prince Henry, who is now referred to as the "Navigator" for his contribution to the exploration efforts of the time. He was monumental in Portugal's early successes in the exploration of the West African coast. Initially, his curiosity did not motivate him. Rather, it was the practical purpose of trying to surround the Muslim Moors of North Africa by the sea from the south, bypassing their lands on the Mediterranean coast. By the time of his death in 1460,

Portugal had managed to expand its reach almost three thousand miles down the African coast, establishing new contacts and largely popularizing the idea that it was possible to reach India by circumnavigating the African continent. The riches accumulated by the Portuguese during this time contributed to a gradual shift of the European maritime power from Italy to Iberia. And Portugal wanted more. The navigating spirit of Prince Henry persisted in Portugal, leading to Bartolomeu Dias's expedition to reach the southern tip of Africa, which was renamed the Cape of Good Hope by King John II, signifying that there was an expectation for more to come in future expeditions.

Columbus

A portrait of Columbus by Sebastiano del Piombo
https://en.wikipedia.org/wiki/File:Portrait_of_a_Man,_Said_to_be_Christopher_Columbus.jpg

Christopher Columbus was a man of Genoese origin. He was fascinated by the idea of exploring the unknown, and he was well versed in navigation and maritime travel. In 1484, he approached Portugal's King John II with his project, the "enterprise of the Indies," proposing the discovery of yet another route to India. However, Columbus proposed sailing in a westward direction. Like most people of the time, Columbus believed the world was spherical, although the idea of traveling west to reach India was met with skepticism. Why should they spend money on an expedition that might never succeed? However, one prominent geographical scholar, Paolo Toscanelli from Florence, and some Portuguese explorers thought islands must exist in the western region of the Atlantic Ocean.

Regardless, Columbus's proposed expedition was rejected by King John II not once but twice. King John was reluctant to agree to finance a new venture to the west when there were already efforts being made to advance Portugal's reach down the West African coast, as this was around the same time that Bartolomeu Dias successfully landed at the Cape of Good Hope. A completely new expedition into the unknown was simply too risky and expensive. In addition to this, Portugal faced financial constraints because of its new rivalry of Portugal with Spain after the marriage of Isabella of Castile and Ferdinand of Aragon united the two kingdoms in 1469. The royal marriage had made Spain a political rival of Portugal, and Spanish ships frequently visited Portuguese possessions in western Africa, threatening to undermine the monopoly of Portuguese trade of African goods. In response to this, Portugal constructed several defensive fortifications along the coast, and the confrontations between the two nations forced them to sign the Treaty of Alcáçovas in 1479. With the treaty, Spain recognized the existing Portuguese possessions, and Portugal recognized the Spanish colony in the Canary Islands.

This somewhat tense relationship between the two Christian Iberian nations was exploited by Christopher Columbus, who traveled to the Spanish court to present his project to Queen Isabella and King Ferdinand in 1492. The Spanish monarchs were charmed by the idea of overtaking Portugal and gaining access to the rich Asian markets by a new route. They recognized that Columbus had a high-risk, high-reward hypothesis and also believed that he might take his case to another power that would be willing to fund the venture and subsequently profit from it. Instead of letting the opportunity go, the Spanish Crown authorized the funding of Columbus's expedition to the Indies, granting the explorer political and commercial rights to claim any new lands for the Crown. The monarchs commissioned three ships for him, two caravels, the *Pinta* and the *Niña*, and one larger carrack, the *Santa María*. In early August 1492, Columbus departed from Andalusia to the Spanish-owned Canary Islands, where he arrived in early September to restock his provisions before heading west.

A little over a month later, the expedition was finally able to spot land in the second week of October. Ecstatic that their journey was a success, the explorers proceeded to explore the islands they had discovered. However, they were not in the Indies or even in the right hemisphere. What they had stumbled upon was The Bahamas. Columbus named the first island he encountered San Salvador before exploring farther and landing on Cuba and Hispaniola (Haiti) by late November.

He described the indigenous peoples he encountered as simple and unskilled in warfare, observing their lack of technology and complexity in their societies. With the help of his interpreter, Luis de Torres, Columbus and his crew made contact with the Taíno, Arawak, and Lucayan peoples, observing their primitive lifestyle and dubbing them *los Indios* ("the Indians"). In Haiti, the explorers founded the settlement of La Navidad in early December, impressing the natives with their large ships and gunpowder before experiencing an accident on the *Santa María* and deciding to return home. While some of the crew stayed in Haiti to set up a permanent base of operations for future ventures, Columbus and most of his men started to sail back in early January 1493, taking some of the natives as prisoners to present to Queen Isabella.

Christopher Columbus managed to make a discovery that would change the course of the world forever. Confident in his triumph, he sailed home, adamant to discuss his achievement with the Spanish Crown.

Later Expeditions

However, on their way back, Columbus and his crew experienced more problems, being forced to land not in Spain but on the Portuguese-controlled island of Santa Maria in the Azores before eventually reaching Lisbon. King John II was notified of his arrival in Lisbon, and the explorer met with the Portuguese king. To King John's disappointment, Columbus showed him the captured natives as proof that he had managed to reach his goal. Although the king stated that the expedition had been a violation of the treaty between Portugal and Spain, he reluctantly let Columbus continue to Spain.

Upon his return, Columbus was hailed as a hero, although there were doubts about whether he had actually managed to reach Asia by traveling west. Some believed he had found an unknown piece of land. When Columbus arrived in The Bahamas, he tried to connect what he found with the existing preconceived notions about Asians. For example, he preemptively applied the name "Indians" to the native population and believed the island of Cuba to have been the island of Cipangu (Japan), which he knew existed somewhere northeast of India.

His actual mistake lay in the fact that he had calculated the earth's circumference to be much smaller than it is. He overestimated the ratio of land to water. Technically, by traveling enough to the west (disregarding the fact that he had a whole unknown continent to cross), he would have ended up in Asia, first encountering the unknown islands that lay northeast of India and Cathay (China). Of course, none of this is actually true. Still, few could have imagined that there was a completely new landmass in the west.

Thanks to the success of the first voyage, a second expedition was commissioned soon after Columbus's arrival in Spain. He set sail from Cadiz in September 1493. This time, Columbus had seventeen ships, much more equipment, and a larger crew. Just like his previous trip, he first arrived at the Canaries and then headed west, though this time, he ended up heading more to the south, landing on the island of Dominica in the Lesser Antilles. From there, the expedition headed northwest to Hispaniola. The explorers found the settlement there destroyed by the natives, leading them to establish a new colony in early 1494 by the name of La Isabela.

During the second expedition, Columbus tried desperately to search for more signs that would indicate that he was in Asia but to no avail. He explored more of the islands of the Caribbean, but over time, he grew to be on bad terms with his crew. A large part of his men died because of disease and the lack of food, and the Spanish no longer got along well with the natives after the latter's attack on La Navidad. Skirmishes broke out between the natives and the colonizers, with Columbus and his men easily overpowering them with their guns. Still, efforts to enter deeper inland on the islands proved unsuccessful, and the colonizers decided to stick to the shores in the safety of their ships before eventually leaving for home in 1496. Throughout their second stay in the New World, Columbus and his crew arrested and killed hundreds of natives, made rough sketches of the island chains in the Caribbean, and took loot they had acquired from the natives.

Upon his arrival in Spain, Columbus realized that he would no longer be the only colonizer to lead expeditions to the west. The royal family had granted the right to explore in the name of the monarchy to other competent people who expressed their desires and provided good plans. For this reason and because word about Columbus's frequent disagreements with his crew had spread throughout the public, it was even more difficult for him to obtain the necessary funds to return to the Indies. When he finally set sail for his third voyage in 1498, his fleet was about half the size it had been five years before.

This time, Columbus divided his expedition into two. He ventured to the south and reached the island of Trinidad near South America, while the bigger party went north to reinforce the colony at Hispaniola. Still, the discontent between the settlers and their clashes with the natives caused great problems, affecting the cohesiveness of the expedition. In October 1499, Columbus sent two ships back to Spain, requesting help from the monarchy to resolve the colonists' issues. The Crown responded by sending a new governor for the colony, a man by the name of Francisco de Bobadilla, who arrived in the New World in October 1500.

Upon de Bobadilla's arrival, he investigated the situation, only to find the camp divided into rival factions. According to his records, Columbus had quarreled with his brothers, Bartholomew and Diego, and was accused of brutally treating the natives and his own men if he suspected them of misconduct. Historians argue whether or not this account of Columbus was correct or if de Bobadilla was motivated by his personal goals to assert his dominance on the island as the representative of the Spanish Crown. Either way, he arrested Columbus and his brothers and sent them back to Spain.

Back home, the Columbus brothers successfully pleaded their case in front of the royal court, saying that de Bobadilla had wrongfully accused them of crimes. Upon hearing this, the court issued an apology to Columbus, and after much consideration, it promised to fund his fourth voyage to the West Indies, which would end up being his last.

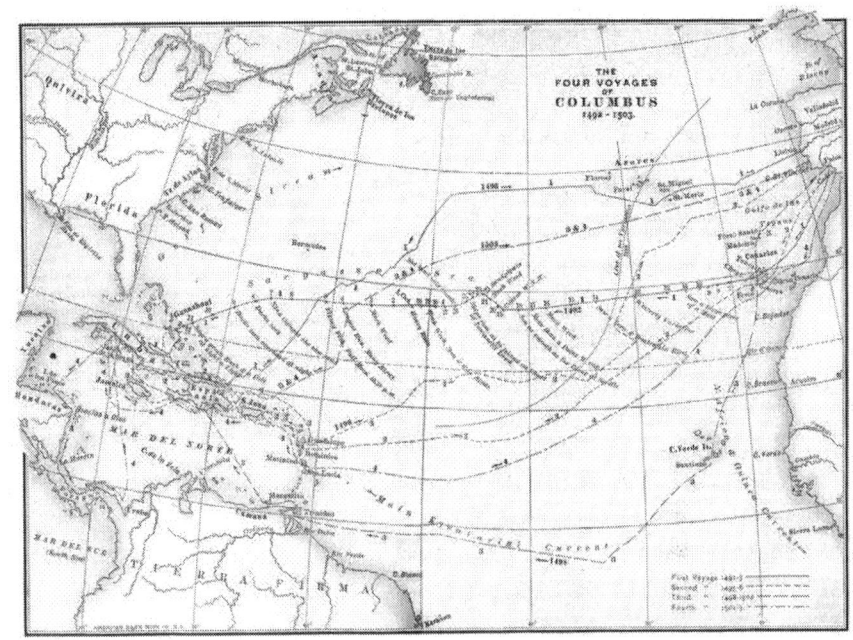

The four voyages of Christopher Columbus.
https://commons.wikimedia.org/wiki/File:The_Four_Voyages_of_Columbus_1492-1503_-_Project_Gutenberg_etext_18571.jpg

Columbus's final expedition would set sail in 1502, but it did not go well for the explorer and his crew. The party was plagued by unfavorable winds and strong storms. The men first arrived at their colony in Hispaniola before moving onto the island of Jamaica. In August 1502, Columbus would finally get to land on a continent, landing in Honduras and exploring the coast south to Nicaragua and Costa Rica for the next few months. After some time, he arrived back in Jamaica in June 1503 but was forced to stay there for longer than he wanted due to the damage his fleet had taken in the expedition.

Columbus was stranded in Jamaica with no help from the colony at Hispaniola, so he was forced to get on good terms with the natives, who supplied the party with provisions to survive for six months, during which time the crew tried to repair the ships to get home. However, the natives soon grew tired of the colonists, as the Spanish had basically nothing valuable left to trade them for food. Columbus used the astrological information he possessed to his advantage, persuading the natives that his God was angry with how they treated the colonists. As punishment, God would make the moon turn red in the following days. Of course, Columbus was speaking of a lunar eclipse, which he was fully aware was going to happen on March 1st, 1504, thanks to the charts his crew possessed. To the horror and astonishment of the natives, Columbus's words came true. Once the explorer declared that God had forgiven the natives after the eclipse had passed, the natives were compelled to continue supplying the colonists with provisions to survive. Finally, after being in Jamaica for a few more months, Columbus and his men were rescued in June and returned to Spain in November of the same year.

Start of the Colonial Race

Christopher Columbus passed away in 1506, just two years after returning home from his final voyage in the West Indies. To his last day, he believed that he had found a western route to the distant waters of Asia, despite all of the overwhelming evidence against it. Still, Columbus was responsible for boosting the drive for exploration in Spain and Portugal. In his lifetime, there were expeditions to the west with the intention of finding out more about the New World and seizing its marvelous riches. However, these voyages were aware of the fact that they were venturing into the unknown, and their outcomes would shape the world in the decades following Columbus's death.

We also have to mention that independent explorers also accidentally reached the Americas soon after Columbus first set foot in The Bahamas. For example, Vicente Yáñez Pinzón landed on the coast of Brazil and explored the northeastern South American coast with an expedition of 1,500 men. Portuguese explorer Pedro Álvares Cabral also landed in Brazil accidentally, but he intended to take a long route southwest of Africa on his way to India. After landing in Brazil, he recalculated his route, realized that he had ended up more west than intended, and recalibrated the course to continue on his way to India, crossing the Atlantic again before reaching the coastal routes of Africa. These voyages followed Vasco da Gama's newly discovered sea route around Africa to India, proving that the discovery of the Americas was inevitable, even if Columbus hadn't traveled westward.

The drive to explore was also boosted by Spain and Portugal's rivalry, as we have already mentioned. The Spanish played the exploration game a bit later than the Portuguese. They recognized that Portuguese interests were mainly concentrated south of Europe in Africa and in the unexplored regions east of it. This notion was further confirmed by Vasco da Gama's successful voyage and increased Portuguese involvement in the trade from India through the Cape of Good Hope. Spain realized that the best course of action was to focus on western exploration, not to challenge the already strong Portuguese holdings in Africa and India. This division seemed natural, especially since the two nations did not know the full extent of the landmass they had discovered, whereas they had a general idea of Africa's size. To make sure that disputes would not arise, the Spanish and the Portuguese decided to resolve the matter with the help of a neutral mediator, an institution that had for a long time assumed a reconciliatory and diplomatic role in international affairs: the papacy.

The papacy was already involved in colonial matters when the two nations approached it in the 1490s. Ever since Portugal had ventured out to Africa, the popes granted the Portuguese monarchs the right to subjugate the non-Christian peoples and spread the word of God in the colonies. Of course, papal involvement was not absolutely necessary in this regard, but since the popes had governed the Christianization of pagans for a long time, it was almost customary for the Portuguese to ask them for permission. In exchange, the papacy granted Portugal gracious donations and missionaries. The Spanish Crown contacted the papacy in 1493 upon the completion of Columbus's first voyage, asking the pope to clear up the ambiguity that might be created with the discovery of new lands.

Papal bulls were issued in 1493, two of which granted the Spanish rights to explore and claim the new lands in the west as long as they spread Catholicism and converted the pagans. The third bull drew an imaginary vertical line in the Atlantic a hundred leagues west of the Cape Verde islands. Any new lands discovered west of this line were granted to the Spanish, while the Portuguese were to keep the possessions east of it. This imaginary division was revised twice until the Treaty of Tordesillas in 1494 finalized it. A new meridian was set up 370 leagues west of the Cape Verde islands to try and divide the Atlantic approximately midway between the Cape Verde islands and the newly discovered West Indies.

Of course, there was no way to accurately calculate this in 1494, and what made the treaty more ambiguous was the fact that most of the New World was not yet discovered. Still, the division was regarded to be good enough by both sides. Although after the colonization of Brazil by Portugal and the establishment of colonies by other European powers, the importance of the treaty slowly diminished, Portugal and Spain mostly followed this arbitrary line for the next few centuries. Because of the Treaty of Tordesillas, Spain was "authorized" to conquer all of central and southwestern America, as well as the islands in the Caribbean, while the Portuguese expanded mostly to the east, with the exception of Brazil.

Before we move on to the history of how Spain managed to conquer the Americas about a hundred years after Columbus first set foot in the West Indies, we have to cover two more important figures of the Age of Exploration, both of whom are very well known today. The first is a Florentine sailor named Amerigo Vespucci—the man after whom the newly discovered continent would eventually be named. Vespucci visited the New World with Columbus during one of his voyages; although he claimed to have first arrived in America in 1497, it is more probable that his earliest visit was in the years between 1499 and 1500. He vividly described the nature and the people that he encountered in his letters, which were subsequently published in Europe in 1503 to the interest of many scholars.

Vespucci was the biggest advocate of the idea that Columbus had discovered a "New World" instead of sailing to the Far East. Vespucci's convincing argument led him to find widespread popularity in Iberia, as the Italian sailed under the flag of both Spain and Portugal, and in the rest of Catholic Europe.

As for the name of the New World, that was thanks to a geographer and a supporter of Vespucci's ideas, Martin Waldseemüller, who encouraged dubbing the New World "America," a feminine name like "Asia" or "Europa." Over time, the name caught on, although the Spanish continued to refer to their colonies as "Los Indios" for a long time.

Another explorer who would forever change the course of history was Ferdinand Magellan, the captain of a Portuguese expedition that was the first to circumnavigate the world by sea between 1519 and 1521. Magellan's plan was similar to that of Columbus, but the Portuguese explorer possessed far more knowledge of the lands lying west of the Atlantic. Magellan set out from Portugal and journeyed south along the coast of South America before eventually heading west through the narrow strait that is now named after him in modern-day Chile. There, he was confronted with the completely unknown Pacific Ocean, the largest body of water in the world. Magellan eventually arrived in the Malay Archipelago, which was called the "Spice Islands" by the Iberians and the eventual place of the Portuguese East Indies. Although Magellan was killed in a clash with the natives in the Philippines, his expedition continued, reaching the African coast and eventually returning to Portugal.

The magnitude of the implications of Magellan's expedition should not be understated. Firstly, it proved that Columbus's theory of getting to Asia by sailing west was right, although the true scale of the world had been grossly understated by the Italian. Secondly, Magellan's trip to the East Indies and his rough map of the world caused the Spanish and the Portuguese to draw a new division line along the 142nd meridian in 1529 with the Treaty of Saragossa. This now meant that Portugal was granted the right to colonize and control the lands east of the Tordesillas line, which included all of Africa, India, and most of Asia, as well as the islands between Australia and Asia all the way to the 142nd meridian. Spain was granted the rights to everything west of the Tordesillas line to the 142nd meridian, which included the Americas and parts of Oceania. Of course, since not everything was discovered at the time and the sizes of the continents and the oceans were not known, neither side knew what exactly fell under their possession. Regardless, the agreement satisfied them both, allowing for clarity and direction for future campaigns.

Finally, Magellan's voyage was a testament that navigation and naval technology were far more advanced than what many had previously thought, although there was room for improvement. It ignited the desire to explore the unknown and come to a better understanding of the New World. By the time Magellan's expedition was completed, military expeditions were already being sent by the Spanish Crown to colonize the New World and bring it under its jurisdiction, but these discoveries only further motivated other Europeans to try their luck at exploration.

The fact of the matter was that Europe was getting a bit too crowded. The Christians were constantly at war with each other without gaining definite results and material gains in most cases. The prospect of a "New World," a mysterious and rich realm that the colonizers knew was inhabited by "inferior" people groups, made it logical to invest in the building of navies and journeys to the unknown. What followed was centuries of colonization, conquest, and exploitation, resulting in the deaths of millions and a complete transformation of the world order.

Chapter Two – Early Conquistador Expeditions

From the Caribbean to the Mainland

Thanks to Columbus's expeditions, the Spanish managed to establish a foothold in the Caribbean, mainly on the island of Hispaniola, with their settlement of La Isabela. In the early 1500s, the colonists mainly focused on strengthening their position in the colonies and maintaining their settlements. This was no easy task since the indigenous population of the Caribbean islands was not always willing to let the foreigners coexist peacefully with them. In part, the hostile relations that developed between the natives and the Spanish were a fault of the early colonizers, including Columbus himself. They never treated the local peoples respectfully, as they recognized early on that they were still too primitive to mount any substantial resistance against European steel armor and guns. Still, the colonizers would sometimes lose men in armed confrontations with the natives. The Europeans' main problem was the lack of manpower, and reinforcing colonies in the early days of colonization was never easy. The colonizers realized this as early as Columbus's second voyage, whose crew found the colony of La Navidad deserted, presumably destroyed by the natives.

In the Caribbean, the local population was more tribal and fragmented. The natives lived in separate agrarian communities and villages. The lack of a united political entity made it easier for the colonizers to subjugate the natives and made it more difficult for the latter to resist. The Spanish look at the natives as inferior, and they imprisoned and forced the natives to work for them, essentially treating them as slaves.

For the colonizers, the New World promised unseen riches, not only in the form of previously unknown foods but also in valuable, rare minerals and metals that could be used to upset the balance in Europe. And since the natives were more knowledgeable about their surroundings than the Spanish and were far weaker than the colonizers, it was only logical for the latter to enslave them for their own means. The indigenous people of the Caribbean islands, not only in Hispaniola but also in Jamaica and The Bahamas, were exploited from very early on. They mined and collected resources for the colonizers and worked under pretty harsh conditions, but they were never referred to as slaves.

This was because of Queen Isabella's decree in 1501, declaring all of the subjugated natives as subjects of the Crown, making it illegal to enslave them. Still, this was very arbitrary, as the natives were still exploited by the *encomienda* system, which the Spanish had utilized to deal with their non-Christian subjects since the days of the Reconquista. During the Reconquista, the Spanish Crown granted the soldiers and commanders who took over Moorish settlements the right to tax and control their conquered subjects. They were essentially entrusted (*encomienda* means "to entrust" in Spanish) the governance of the non-Christian people. Over the years, the system developed, and as the colonizers reached the New World, royal grants were issued to them to be applied to the indigenous American peoples. In 1503, the Crown officially issued the *encomienda* grants to the *encomendero* colonizers, subjecting the natives in a given area to the *encomendero* and his successors. Technically, according to the law, the *encomenderos* were not to come into possession of the land assigned to them for governance, although they essentially had unrestricted control over them.

The *encomienda* system matured and changed over the years, staying in use until 1720, when a royal decree officially abolished it. Throughout more than two hundred years, the royal grantees were basically the all-powerful governors of the native population of the Americas, exploiting them for labor and forcing them to pay tribute. The system was so exploitative that it resulted in the deaths of countless indigenous communities at the hands of the Spanish. Forced labor and new rules disrupted the agrarian lifestyles of the natives, leading to lower agricultural yields, which caused famine throughout their villages. Of course, we also have to mention that coming into direct contact with foreigners from such a remote land meant the natives contracted several previously unknown diseases from the Europeans due to their lack of immunity. As more and more colonizers flocked into the New World, searching for wealth, glory, and adventure, the number of natives slowly began to decrease, with hundreds of thousands of them dying from non-warfare-related issues.

Still, for the first two decades of the 16th century, Spanish colonial activity was limited to the Caribbean islands, as the colonizers were not yet ready to move on to colonizing continental America. Throughout this time, efforts were made to better explore their surroundings and find out the true scale of the landmass that lay west of the first colonial settlements on Hispaniola. The need to explore also came from the fact that the Spanish were unable to find the wealth and resources in the Caribbean on the scale they had expected from Columbus's journeys.

From the explorations of the early 16th century, they slowly became aware they had encountered the least developed Native American societies on the Caribbean islands, as the explorers who landed in the Yucatán Peninsula and sailed down the coast to the Isthmus of Panama brought reports of much wealthier and greater civilizations. Once the Spanish were able to expand their territorial gains and found more colonies, they slowly came into contact with these civilizations. They wanted to gain control of their magnificent cities and great riches, so they started to organize more and more military campaigns against them. Before that, the activities of the Spanish in the Caribbean cannot quite be referred to as "conquests," especially when we compare them with what the colonizers did on the American mainland, although armed encounters certainly did break out between the colonizers and the natives there. Beginning in the 1510s, the Spanish conquest of the Americas truly kicked off, resulting in the subjugation and outright destruction of millions of people.

Early Expeditions to Central America

One of the first colonizers to explore continental Central America was Bartholomew Columbus in the year 1502. He arrived with his crew at the small island of Guanaja, which lies off the coast of modern-day Honduras. There, he encountered and seized a large wooden canoe full of natives. These people were the Maya, an advanced civilization that mostly inhabited the Yucatán Peninsula in Central America. The canoe also carried valuable materials like cotton textiles, cocoa, and metal tools and weapons, which were taken by the colonizers. Bartholomew and his men noticed that the canoe had approached from the west, indicating that there was human life in that direction, although they chose not to explore further.

About nine years later, in 1511, a group of Spanish sailors ended up on the coast of the Yucatán after being caught in a storm in the Caribbean. Led by Pedro de Valdivia, the colonizers were captured by a local Maya lord, and most of them were sacrificed and eaten. Only two sailors from the group managed to escape captivity, fleeing to a neighboring tribe from Chetumal, which was hostile toward the chief they had just escaped from. After being initially enslaved by the Maya, one of them, Gonzalo Guerrero, managed to eventually gain the trust of the natives and was given the rank of a commanding officer in their army. Interestingly, both survivors would ultimately make contact with the Spanish conquistadors several years later after the latter had arrived in the Yucatán to conquer the Aztec Empire.

The first Spanish expedition that really explored the Yucatán Peninsula and had significant contact with the natives was the one led by Francisco Hernández de Córdoba, which set sail from a Spanish colony in Cuba in 1517. Intending to primarily gain a better understanding of the region, the expedition arrived on the northeastern coast of the Yucatán in early 1517 but could not land at first due to shallow waters. However, they were able to spot the settlements on land, and due to the pyramids they could see from the ships, they dubbed the place Gran Cairo, which literally translates to Great Cairo. This was probably the town of El Meco, north of modern-day Cancún. On the following day, the colonizers were approached by the local Maya, who sailed in several large canoes. The Maya were invited on board, and the two parties exchanged gifts. Córdoba asked their leader to take them to land, and the Maya returned the next day with additional canoes to carry the Spaniards to the shore, where they were met with tens of locals who were curious to see the foreigners. The Spanish named the coast Cape Catoche.

To their surprise, they were ambushed by the locals once they made their way to the town. The natives managed to kill and wound about ten of the crew before the Spanish were able to regroup and retreat, pillaging the town's buildings on their way. In the end, Córdoba and his men managed to escape to the ships, having captured two locals and taken some golden items from the Maya city. The abundance of gold in the Maya settlement, as well as the use of other metals and materials for decorative purposes, indicated to the Spanish that they would soon find the promised riches of the New World.

Córdoba's expedition continued west along the coast and around the tip of the Yucatán. He and his men encountered the natives on several occasions and engaged in armed skirmishes during each of them. It seemed that these people groups were far more hostile than the ones in the Caribbean, and they were also more advanced than those who had been living under the Spanish *encomienda* system for more than fifteen years. The colonizers also noted more towns on the coast, like the Maya city of Campeche, which they dubbed San Lázaro because it was spotted on St. Lazarus's Day. The Spanish were actually permitted to land and make contact with its inhabitants, observing their rituals before eventually having to fight with the natives again.

Captain Córdoba was wounded in one of the clashes with the natives, forcing the expedition to sail back to Cuba. In fact, the continuous armed confrontations with the Maya severely depleted the number of Spanish, who lost more than half of their men and had several wounded. The lack of men caused them to abandon one of their ships because it was impossible to man it. After a short detour, during which the expedition landed in Florida to restock their water provisions, the party managed to return to Cuba. Francisco Hernández de Córdoba passed away soon after his arrival due to the wounds he had suffered. Cuba's governor, Diego Velázquez, proceeded to interrogate the captured Natives, who said to the colonizers that there was a lot of gold to be found in Yucatán.

The Aztecs

Upon the arrival of de Córdoba's expedition, Governor Velázquez was adamant about finding the promised haven of gold in the west, so he commissioned another expedition consisting of 240 men and 4 ships under Juan de Grijalva in 1518. Leaving Cuba in the spring of 1518, the colonizers first landed east of the Yucatán at the island of Cozumel and then proceeded south along the peninsula's eastern coast. Then, the expedition changed course in early May, going north and circling the tip of the peninsula before sailing southwest along its coast. The Spanish spotted many Maya cities from their ships but rarely made contact with the natives, knowing the hostilities that had erupted between them and other colonizers before.

Still, they would be forced to confront the Maya at Campeche and Champoton, the places where Córdoba's men had been attacked by the natives. This time, the colonizers were wise not to leave their ships and instead fired at the approaching canoes from the safety of their vessels.

After sailing around the peninsula, the colonizers eventually arrived at the mouth of the Tabasco River, which would eventually be renamed after Grijalva. There, they were able to barter with the locals and gain information about the great empire of the Aztecs, which was supposedly located to the west and was rich in gold. Motivated by the stories of the natives at the Tabasco River, the expedition continued along the coast to the north, reaching the mouth of the Panuco before heading back to Cuba to relay the information they had gathered.

Grijalva's expedition provided the colonizers with better knowledge of Central America's coastline and the riches of the Aztecs, prompting the Spanish to start preparing for more expeditions to explore the unknown. A year later, an expedition of about five hundred men and eleven ships set out from Cuba, and this expedition would change the course of history forever. It was headed by Hernán Cortés, a Spaniard who had dwelled in the New World since 1504 and had good relations with Governor Velázquez. Cortés and his men were the first true colonizers to start actively conquering the peoples they met upon their arrival in Central America, making them, for all intents and purposes, the first conquistadors.

Before we move on to Cortés and his infamous campaigns against the Aztecs, we have to say a few words about the Aztec Empire, an empire that was shrouded in mystery in 1519 when the conquistadors first set out to find out more about it. Our knowledge of the Aztecs derives from the accounts of the European colonizers, who extensively described them in their chronicles, and from various archaeological discoveries which indicate the amazing scale of their existence in Mesoamerica (not to forget the modern descendants of the Aztecs who still speak the language and have modified their lives in accordance with the changing times since the arrival of the Europeans about five centuries earlier).

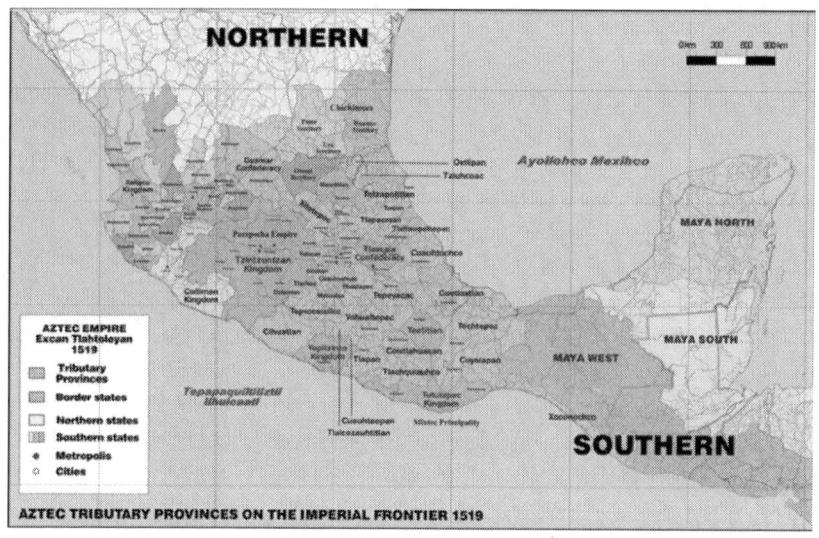

A look at the Aztec Empire in 1519.
Giggette, CC BY-SA 3.0 <https://creativecommons.org/licenses/by-sa/3.0>, via Wikimedia Commons; https://commons.wikimedia.org/wiki/File:Territorial_Organization_of_the_Aztec_Empire_1519.png

The Aztecs, like all other Native American peoples, are thought to have migrated from Asia about thirty thousand years ago. To this day, they remain one of the most advanced native societies in the Americas. The Aztecs primarily inhabited the Valley of Mexico and its surrounding regions. They succeeded the Chichimeca and the Toltec inhabitants of the valley around 1300. In the 14th century, the Aztecs founded their great city of Tenochtitlan, the site of modern Mexico City.

An illustration of what Tenochtitlan might have looked like.
Gary Todd from Xinzheng, China, CC0, via Wikimedia Commons; https://commons.wikimedia.org/wiki/File:Painting_of_Tenochtitlan-Tlatelolco_on_Lake_Texcoco_(9755215791).jpg

Tenochtitlan was an incredible example of Mesoamerican culture and demonstrated the greatness of the Aztecs. The city was built on an artificial island in a lake, making it difficult for hostile peoples in the area to attack. Soon after, the Aztecs developed an iconic military tradition, being known by their neighbors as fierce warriors. The Aztecs managed to subjugate most of their neighbors and created an empire, a confederation of powerful city-states that answered to the emperor in Tenochtitlan.

Thus, the Aztecs became the overlords of the region in the span of about two hundred years, with the peak of their empire coinciding with the beginning of the 16th century and the arrival of the colonizers in the Americas. By the time Cortés and his men made their way through Mesoamerica to the lands of the Aztecs, the native peoples on the coast of the Gulf of Mexico were already under Aztec control, with the true power of the empire lying in the heart of the Valley of Mexico around Lake Texcoco.

Of course, Cortés and his men were not aware of the strength and the overall nature of the Aztec Empire, but they were curious to find out what the mysterious empire in the west had in store for them and their cannons.

Chapter Three – The Conquest of the Aztec Empire

Setting Sail

Today, the infamous story of Cortés's campaign against the Aztecs is well known as one of the clearest examples of Spanish domination over the indigenous peoples. However, few people are aware of the fact that the expedition had rough beginnings, something that stemmed from personal quarrels between Cortés and Governor Velázquez of Cuba. In the early days of colonization, it was difficult to obtain local funding for expeditions, as they were very expensive endeavors that did not always yield profits for the Spanish Crown. Therefore, Cortés, a former lawyer-turned-colonizer, had to work hard to obtain the right to have the expedition commissioned by Governor Velázquez, which he finally managed to do in October 1518.

However, although Velázquez provided the conquistador with six hundred men and eleven ships, he strictly told Cortés to only explore and establish contact with the Aztecs to potentially set up trade between the rich empire and the Spanish West Indies. It is suspected that the governor intended to lead a following expedition into the Aztec lands to be the one associated with its conquest.

Although we don't know the true reason behind Velázquez's decision to limit Cortés's mission, we do know the latter definitely was not content with the governor. Cortés convinced his men that Velázquez wanted the glory and the riches that the expedition promised for himself, earning their trust and setting sail from Santiago de Cuba. Velázquez's efforts to intercept him failed, so technically speaking, Cortés was acting on his own interests, independently from the orders from the representative of the Crown, making him and his men mutineers. However, once they were out of Cuba, there was no way for the governor to catch them, leaving Cortés in charge of one of the most daring colonial campaigns.

A painting of Cortés.
https://en.wikipedia.org/wiki/File:Retrato_de_Hern%C3%A1n_Cort%C3%A9s.jpg

The expedition set out in early 1519 and soon reached the island of Cozumel off the coast of the Yucatán. They made contact with the natives and were informed of two similar-looking men who lived in one of the tribes on the peninsula, prompting Cortés to send messengers to inquire about them. Sure enough, the men the natives were talking about were the two explorers from the 1511 expedition—Gonzalo Guerrero and Gerónimo de Aguilar. Cortés invited them to join his crew, and Aguilar accepted. Since he had mastered the local Nahuatl language, he agreed to become Cortés's interpreter. Guerrero respectfully declined, telling Cortés that he had a family to take care of and an important position in the tribe as one of the chief warriors. Thus, Cortés left Cozumel, taking a Spaniard with him who had been living among the natives for nearly eight years.

The expedition then advanced northwest along the coast, circling the tip of the peninsula and arriving at the city of Potonchan, which was located on the left bank of the Tabasco River. Aware that the city had gold, Cortés engaged in combat with the natives and defeated them twice before looting the city and taking many natives as prisoner. Most importantly, Cortés met a Nahua woman by the name of La Malinche or Malintzin, whom he took as a captive and Christened her Marina. Dona Marina, as she would come to be eventually referred to by the Spanish, became another interpreter, as she was more familiar with the Aztec dialect of the Nahuatl language than Aguilar. Due to her approachable nature and knowledge, she advised the conquistadors throughout the Aztec campaign and grew close to Cortés, ultimately developing an intimate relationship with the colonizer and bearing him his first son, Martín.

The March to Tenochtitlan

The expedition continued, landing at what is now the Mexican province of Veracruz in April 1519. Reportedly, soon after the landing, Cortés came across the first Aztec messengers sent by Emperor Moctezuma II. The Aztecs had no intention of hostilities, greeting the Spanish with gifts and hoping to maintain good relations with them. It is likely the Aztecs were already aware of the military capabilities of the conquistadors.

While in Veracruz, the conquistadors founded the settlement of Villa Rica de la Vera Cruz, which became the modern-day Mexican city of Veracruz. The main reason behind this is thought to have been Cortés's attempt to legitimize himself since he had defied royal orders upon his departure from Cuba.

To do this, Cortés and his men organized a local council, a *cabildo*, which, according to the Spanish legislation, elected him as the *adelantado*, essentially granting him the powers of a governor and chief justice. As an appointed *adelantado*, Cortés was legally free from the authority of Diego Velázquez since Villa Rica was not under the latter's jurisdiction of Cuba.

Since Cortés needed royal permission to have a legal position, he ordered a few of his crewmen to sail to Spain to obtain recognition from King Charles V. To convince the Crown of his successes, Cortés gave them the loot obtained from Potonchan. Among the delegation was Francisco de Montejo, a conquistador who would eventually play a big role in the conquest of the Yucatán. This decision is one of the examples of the arbitrary nature of existing rules in the early days of colonization. Cortés was fully aware of the legal complications and tried to exploit those weaknesses to cement himself as a powerful figure in the New World.

As Cortés continued his march, moving with his fellow conquistadors little by little inland, he encountered several native settlements, which he found out were tributaries of the Aztec Empire. The Spanish soon came to realize that the Aztecs had subjugated these people against their will and heavily taxed them, resulting in the hostile attitudes of many natives. Cortés used this to his advantage, convincing the natives to rise up against their Aztec masters on his way to the capital city of Tenochtitlan.

Having the tributary peoples on his side allowed Cortés to establish his foothold in Mexico relatively easily. When he had to fight against the unwelcoming natives, he peacefully released prisoners to demonstrate that he was friendly. At Cempoala, for example, Cortés imprisoned the Aztec tax collectors who governed the tributary city for the empire, and in Tlaxcala, he convinced the local warlord to ally with him against Moctezuma after defeating him in battle.

The march to the Aztec capital of Tenochtitlan continued throughout the summer and early autumn of 1519, and thanks to the diplomatic efforts of Cortés, the conquistadors did not lose many men to the natives on their way. In fact, the natives offered presents to the Spanish, who promised them liberation from the Aztecs, and they were also relatively receptive to Christianity. For example, at Tlaxcala, an independent city-state enclave in the Aztec-controlled lands east of Tenochtitlan, the locals were happy to add the Christian God of the conquistadors to their polytheistic pantheon. The daughters of local elders were baptized and given Christian names. Tlaxcalan warriors even joined Cortés's expedition, continuing the journey west through the city of Cholula.

Cholula was one of the largest cities under Aztec control. It was mainly a religious site, so it held immense importance. The Aztec messengers, who tried to get on good terms with the conquistadors and dissuade them from journeying to Tenochtitlan, persuaded Cortés to make the journey to Tenochtitlan through Cholula. The Tlaxcalans and the Cempaoalans who accompanied Cortés had warned him to take an alternate route, but the conquistador was adamant about seeing the religious city himself.

When the Spanish arrived in the city, they were not greeted with friendship. Cholula did not have a large army, and Cortés decided not to order his troops to attack and planned to leave the city and proceed to Tenochtitlan. However, on the third day, his advisor, Dona Marina, talked with one of the wives of the city's chiefs. She informed Cortés that the Aztecs planned to ambush the Spanish at Cholula and had conspired with Cholula's leaders, telling them not to provide the conquistadors with provisions. It is unclear whether or not an Aztec ambush was being prepared, but Cortés ordered his men to strike preemptively against the natives of Cholula.

The battle that ensued has rightfully been dubbed the "Massacre of Cholula" since the city's population was no match for the conquistadors and their weapons. The Spanish fought ruthlessly, storming the holy temples and pyramids, capturing the city's nobility, and cutting their way through the resistance. Thousands of natives were killed at Cholula, and the city was almost completely reduced to ruins, with the conquistadors taking all the valuables they could. The Great Pyramid of Cholula, rising in the center of the city, was almost fully destroyed, and the Spanish put a cross on top of it to signal the triumph of Christianity over the pagan natives.

There are several different accounts of why the massacre took place, each containing different versions of the ambush against the conquistadors or the ruthlessness of Cortés. Nevertheless, the grim fate of Cholula probably served as an example to other neighboring cities to cooperate with the Spanish rather than resist them. Perhaps this was the reason behind Emperor Moctezuma's decision to invite the conquistadors to Tenochtitlan. Days after razing the holy city to the ground, Cortés met with messengers from the Aztec emperor, who probably realized there was no use in trying to stop the foreigners and was compelled to invite the conquistadors to his capital on his own terms.

Arriving at Tenochtitlan

The conquistadors were more than happy to accept the emperor's invitation and arrived at the gates of Tenochtitlan in November 1519. The city was a thriving megapolis and, if the reports of the Spanish are to be believed, one of the largest cities in the world. The Aztec capital dazzled the colonizers. Built on an island in Lake Texcoco, the city was not surrounded by high walls since the water acted as a natural barrier to potential enemies. Tenochtitlan was connected to the land by a couple of bridges, which were wide enough for only a carriage to pass. A product of outstanding urban planning, the different residential and public areas inside the city were carefully interwoven with each other, with marketplaces and rectangular temples built in stone scattered throughout. In the center was a large square with the city's main pyramid, where most of the rituals and ceremonies took place. Alongside the many temples, each dedicated to different deities, there was also the grand palace of the emperor, with a hundred rooms and baths and golden decorations. Overall, Tenochtitlan was unlike anything the Spanish had seen. It was a true jewel of the Mesoamerican civilization.

The conquistadors were greeted at the entrance of the city by Emperor Moctezuma II himself, who was accompanied by several other important figures, including the kings of the allied city-states of Texcoco, Tlacopan, and Tlatelolco. All of them were lavishly decorated with feathers and golden jewelry, wearing colorful attire that signaled their status. Many locals watched as their emperor met with Cortés, who presented himself as the representative of the Spanish Crown and praised the Aztec emperor. Interestingly, to demonstrate his friendliness, Cortés wished to embrace Moctezuma but was denied the request by the emperor's accompaniers, as no one was allowed to touch him. Despite this, Cortés and his men were treated very well by the Aztec emperor and were given good quarters to stay in during their visit. Cortés was allowed to stay in the Axayacatl palace.

What transpired next between the conquistador commander and the Aztec emperor is still partially shrouded in mystery, but the developments after Cortés's arrival in Tenochtitlan soon led to him controlling Moctezuma and, by default, his empire for nearly a year. There are several accounts of what happened. According to one of them, Moctezuma held a private audience with Cortés on the day of his arrival, where he supposedly praised and paid respects to the conquistador, believing that he was the promised incarnation of the deity Quetzalcoatl. Quetzalcoatl was one of the central gods of the Aztecs and was depicted as a giant feathered green serpent and the god of life and wisdom. Cortés resembled the description of the awaited incarnation of Quetzalcoatl in the Aztec myths with his light skin and beard. He was supposedly the god who had promised to come to the Aztecs from the east. This was the reason behind Moctezuma treating him as his and his people's savior and pledging to serve him forever.

This narrative was held to be true for many years after the conquest of the Aztecs, but recent scholarship has challenged it because of its suspicious origins. Only the Spanish sources tell of Cortés being perceived as a promised deity; there is no real evidence of the legend about the return of Quetzalcoatl. So, it is likely that Moctezuma did not outright offer his throne and control of his empire to the conquistador because he thought Cortés was a god. Some scholars have argued that if the Aztec emperor was humble enough, he offered control to show his status to Cortés, as politeness and hospitality in the Aztec culture might have been a tool to assert dominance.

The private meeting between the two did happen, but it is more likely that Cortés convinced Moctezuma to rule as his puppet emperor without the latter necessarily regarding him as a god. Cortés likely coerced or threatened the Aztec emperor, reminding him of how he had destroyed other natives on his way to Tenochtitlan. In addition, the conquistador appears to have not undermined the authority of Moctezuma publicly, as the latter was basically forced to accept his new suzerain from behind the scenes while maintaining his position as the most important person in the empire.

In any case, soon after the arrival of the conquistadors in Tenochtitlan, Emperor Moctezuma was essentially a secret prisoner of Cortés, fearing his display of military might and thinking that if he resisted, he would meet the same end as the nobles in Cholula. It is not impossible that the emperor made up the story of the returning promised deity from the east to justify his decision to his subjects.

La Noche Triste

Thus, for nearly half a year after the arrival of the conquistadors at Tenochtitlan, the conquistadors enjoyed almost complete freedom in the Aztec capital. Even though the Aztec emperor was forced to pay large amounts of tribute to the Spanish every month, the conquistadors did not refrain from exploring the surroundings of Tenochtitlan to find more gold and other valuables. They went as far south as Tuxtepec, trying to get more accurate maps and study the area. In Tenochtitlan, Cortés and his missionaries managed to slowly spread Christianity among the people, which was endorsed by Moctezuma, although they did not force the religion on the Aztecs.

The situation changed drastically in April 1520 when Cortés was informed of a new conquistador expedition that had just landed at Veracruz. Cuba's governor, Diego Velázquez, had finally managed to gather enough funds to establish a bigger expedition. Pánfilo de Narvaez, a trustee of Velázquez, set out from Cuba with nineteen ships and more men than Cortés. Velázquez had decided to put an end to Cortés and his defiance of orders, sending Narvaez to take him and his crew as prisoner and seize the riches they had gathered.

Storms and logistical difficulties delayed Narvaez's expedition, resulting in the loss of six of his ships and an overall incohesive campaign. Despite this, he managed to overpower the natives at Cempoala, capturing the city. Having heard of the newly arrived conquistadors who challenged his and his men's position as the self-declared masters of the Aztecs, Cortés prepared to sally out from Tenochtitlan and confront Narvaez.

Cortés set out from the Aztec capital in mid-May. He knew he would be outnumbered, so he sent messengers to a friendly nearby tribe. The messengers returned with a couple of hundred natives, reinforcing the army. In late May, as Cortés approached Cempoala, he ordered a surprise assault on the city, catching its Spanish defenders off-guard and quickly seizing their artillery. In the battle that ensued, Narvaez was wounded in the eye, and his men soon surrendered to Cortés, who allowed them to join his ranks instead of going back to Cuba. Narvaez's surviving crew agreed and switched sides, convinced by Cortés' argument. Having dealt with the problem and leaving Cempoala in the hands of the natives, Cortés and his men started their march back to Tenochtitlan.

However, upon their return, Cortés found that a fight had broken out between the men he had left behind in the city under Pedro de Alvarado and the locals on May 22nd. The confrontation took place at the Great Temple, where the natives had planned to celebrate their annual religious festival of Toxcatl. The festival was supposed to honor the Aztec god Tezcatlipoca. Its central ceremony included a ritualistic sacrifice of a young man at the temple.

The Spanish and the Aztec accounts of what transpired in the absence of Cortés vary. The conquistadors claimed they were appalled by the festival's ruthless nature and wanted to stop the sacrifice, while the Aztec narrative states that the foreigners simply desired to get a hold of the golden objects that were on display during the festival. Still, whatever the reason, the two sides got in a tussle with each other during the procession of the ritual, and Alvarado ordered his men to preemptively attack the gathered people as a show of force. Acting on their captain's orders, the conquistadors opened fire at the Great Temple, killing many nobles and forcing the ceremony to be abandoned. When Cortés got back to the city in late June, Alvarado justified his actions by saying that the Aztecs had planned to retake power during his absence by striking at his men.

In any case, as word spread about the massacre in the Great Temple, the Aztecs became increasingly hostile toward the Spanish. As people who placed immense value on their culture, beliefs, and religion, the response of the natives was fully justified. The upset population of Tenochtitlan took to the streets, arming themselves and laying siege to the palace where Cortés was staying with the emperor. Fierce fighting ensued between the conquistadors and the locals. Although the Spanish possessed better weapons, they were heavily outnumbered, making it impossible to put up a good fight against tens of thousands of Aztecs. According to Spanish accounts, Emperor Moctezuma tried to subdue the hostile population but was wounded during one of the attacks and died soon after.

Desperate, Cortés decided that the best course of action was to flee the city. He ordered his men to gather whatever wealth they could and devised a plan to escape at nightfall through the western causeway over the lake, which would lead his men to the town of Tlacopan.

On the night of July 1st, 1520, Cortés gave the order, and the conquistadors sallied out from the palace with all the gold they could carry, hurrying to the western causeway. Burdened by their loot, heavy armor, and equipment and making their way through a terrible rainstorm, many conquistadors fell while fighting the natives, who were caught off-guard by the bold move of Cortés and his men. They had to fight their way through the elite Eagle Warrior contingents of the Aztecs, sustaining many losses and injuries but still somehow crossing the causeway. Aiding the conquistadors were their ally natives, hundreds of whom also died fighting their subjugators.

After several stressful hours, Cortés finally had time to regroup on the western coast of the lake, having escaped the main Aztec forces and destroying the causeway. He suffered an injury himself. The conquistador commander had a gruesome task in front of him since he had lost almost all of the progress he had made over the past year. La Noche Triste, or the Sad Night, as the day came to be known, marked the expulsion of the conquistadors from Tenochtitlan and the reclamation of the capital by the Aztecs.

Stalemate

The surviving conquistadors who fled from Tenochtitlan eventually ended up in Tlaxcala with the allied natives. They did not stop their retreat for days, as they were afraid that the Aztec soldiers would catch up to them. Eventually, they were forced to fight with them on the plains of Otumba. Although the Spanish were able to fight off the Aztecs with the help of their Tlaxcalan allies, they still sustained heavy losses and were forced to abandon most of their weapons to escape.

After arriving at Tlaxcala, Cortés was able to assess the damage that had been done. Only a small part of the Spanish crew had survived, and had it not been for the reinforcements the conquistadors received from Narvaez's expedition, they would have all perished. They had also lost almost all of their horses and artillery equipment, which had allowed them to take the edge over their opponents in previous encounters. True, the conquistadors did take whatever valuables they could, but it was nothing compared to what had been available to them in Tenochtitlan. Wounded and demotivated, they sought help from the locals in Tlaxcala and reconsidered their plan of action.

Cortés knew that he had little time and that retreat was not an option. He was still an enemy of the Cuban governor, so he could not risk returning to the Caribbean, despite having the loot his men had amassed as evidence that he had made his way to the Aztec Empire. The conquistador's mind was preoccupied with the thought of conquering Tenochtitlan. But with the number of men at his disposal, it seemed literally impossible. Getting into the city would be extremely difficult, let alone holding it against its hostile population. Cortés decided to ask the other natives for help against the Aztecs.

By the time of his retreat to Tlaxcala in mid-July of 1520, he was fully aware of the fact that the Aztec Empire had been forged in warfare. The Aztecs had subjugated neighboring tribes by force and instilled fear in the people, making them grow increasingly hostile. Thus, it was only logical for Cortés to exploit the unfriendly relations between the different peoples under Aztec suzerainty. He hoped that he had enough men to take Tenochtitlan for himself.

For nearly a year, as the remaining conquistadors licked their wounds, Cortés and his men got to work. The Tlaxcalans were their main allies, although they had already contributed many men to the Spanish cause. So, when Cortés approached their elders once again for support, they made demands in return for providing more soldiers. The Tlaxcalans mainly wanted not to be disregarded in case the campaign against Tenochtitlan proved to be successful; they wanted to share the spoils of war with the Spanish and be exempt from tribute. Cortés, who was short-handed in the negotiations, agreed to all of their demands, promising they would be upheld if they succeeded in capturing Tenochtitlan.

With the native soldiers from Tlaxcala secured, Cortés and his conquistadors then turned to other smaller tributary tribes of the Aztecs and either convinced them to rise up against Tenochtitlan or forced them to switch sides after defeating them in battle. Cortés even managed to get the city-state of Texcoco on his side, which was one of the three city-states in the main Aztec confederation alongside Tenochtitlan and Tlacopan. He was able to achieve this by helping the brother of the *tlatoani* (ruler) of Texcoco, Ixtlilxochitl, in his succession dispute with Cacamatzin, who was supported by the Aztecs. With help from the inside, Cortés and his forces entered Texcoco and declared Ixtlilxochitl the new *tlatoani*, earning his support and strengthening their position. Texcoco was a valuable city because it lay very close to Tenochtitlan on the eastern side of the lake. This provided the conquistadors with access to the lake, prompting them to start building ships for an amphibious assault on the city.

Cortés's plan to sway the natives on his side proved to be very successful, and by the next spring, he had tens of thousands of native soldiers in his army from Texcoco, Tlaxcala, Cholula, and other city-states. This significantly swung the tides of the upcoming battle in favor of the Spanish. Not only that, but Cortés also received significant conquistador reinforcements too. In this regard, the leader of the expedition got lucky, as the men sent to Central America from the West Indies were intended to either reinforce Narvaez or explore the northern part of Mexico independently of Cortés. However, upon their arrival, the Spaniards found that Cortés was amassing a huge army to take the Aztec capital, meaning that joining him promised gold and glory. They were easily convinced to help him in the upcoming battle. Cortés also got more men from the abandoned expeditions commissioned by the

Jamaican governor to explore the Panuco River. Instead of going to the unknown, these conquistadors were invited by Cortés to join his ranks, providing him with artillery, guns, and crossbows that would be needed to overpower the Aztecs.

However, there was another factor that helped Cortés consolidate his position and amass a huge army for Tenochtitlan. After fleeing from the city, the conquistadors had been relatively safe from the Aztecs, as the latter did not send any armies to expel them from their lands once and for all. This was because of an outbreak of smallpox in the capital, which decimated the Aztec population and completely paralyzed the city. As we have already mentioned, the Aztecs and other natives had no immunity to smallpox or to other European diseases. It is likely they contracted the deadly disease from one of the Spanish conquistadors in Tenochtitlan, who had probably been left behind during La Noche Triste. Smallpox, whose name from the native language of Nahuatl roughly translates to "great rash," spreads very quickly in large populations through coughing and sneezing. By early 1521, smallpox had destroyed Tenochtitlan and its population. The disease also spread to other Aztec-controlled areas through human contact.

In total, it is estimated that half of the city's population perished before Cortés amassed his forces to launch an assault on the city in late May 1521, with most people, especially infants and children, dying outright from the disease. Countless others were weakened to the point of exhaustion, and their inability to pursue agriculture and other day-to-day activities caused famine, which also contributed to the instability in Tenochtitlan not a year after the expulsion of the conquistadors. In short, the epidemic greatly compromised the Aztecs' position. Smallpox was contracted by almost everyone, including the emperor after Moctezuma, Cuitláhuac. The new *tlatoani*, Cuauhtémoc, did not have much to work with when he became emperor in early 1521 since most of the population had been decimated by the plague. This is why he was unable to mount any resistance to the approaching conquistador threat, leaving Cortés and his large army unopposed.

The Fall of the Aztec Empire

By the spring of 1521, Cortés had managed to convince most of the tributaries of the Aztecs to rise up against Tenochtitlan and provide him with men for an assault on the city. Most of the tribes, as we have already mentioned, were more than happy to cooperate, so when the conquistador commander was finally ready to launch his offensive on the Aztec capital, he had more men at his disposal than he could have imagined. It is difficult to say the exact number since the sources are conflicting, but it is safe to estimate that as many as 100,000 natives joined Cortés from different settlements by May. With the support of the locals, Cortés relocated to Texcoco from Tlaxcala, as it provided a safer and closer base of operations. There, he ordered his men to start building ships for the upcoming siege.

By then, Cortés was an experienced commander when it came to fighting the Aztecs. He knew that despite his advantage of the guns and crossbows, which were far more powerful weapons than what the enemy could field, it simply was not enough to break the Aztecs at Tenochtitlan. They were fierce warriors and unafraid to face the Spanish guns. They would charge right at them, and they had already shown great valor in the previous battles. Cortés probably had about a thousand Spanish at best, so the best course of action was to divide his large army into smaller contingents and let groups of conquistadors act as elite corps. Cortés was also aware of the fact that carrying a successful direct assault on Tenochtitlan would be very difficult since the city was only connected to the mainland by several causeway bridges, which could easily be destroyed. That is why building ships in Texcoco and mounting an amphibious assault was necessary, as the attackers could land at different points inside the city and fight their way through.

After getting Texcoco on their side, Cortés and his men managed to build thirteen small sloops. The sloops were fast and great for covering short distances. Although they were small compared to other European ships that typically sailed the seas, the Aztec canoes could do no harm to them.

The complete blockade of Tenochtitlan remained the main strategy. The conquistador commander wanted to cut off the city, which had already been badly affected by the plague, from outside supplies and weaken it before mounting a final offensive.

In May 1521, the conquistadors were ready. The first encounters between the attacking contingents and the Aztec defenders happened when Spanish forces under Pedro de Alvarado and Cristóbal de Olid approached Tenochtitlan by foot from the west. Their main objective was cutting the city off from its main water supply at Chapultepec, but the twenty thousand or so attacking soldiers were confronted by Aztec forces that sallied out from Tlacopan before they could seize the town. In the ensuing battle, the Aztecs were able to push the attackers back.

Meanwhile, Aztec canoes sailed toward Cortés's ships, trying to destroy them before they could reach Tenochtitlan, but to no avail. Still, Spanish records show that Lake Texcoco was apparently full of traps and defensive mechanisms like wooden spikes and holes to prevent the Spanish sloops from reaching the capital easily. Additionally, as the conquistadors tried to take control of the northern and western causeways of Tenochtitlan, they were turned back by the defenders, who reinforced their positions once the fighting for the bridges ended at night.

In June, as the conquistadors launched another assault to try and take Tlatelolco, they found themselves ambushed and were defeated after fierce fighting in the northern part of Tenochtitlan. Pedro de Alvarado sustained a wound but managed to retreat with most of his men, but thousands of allied natives and tens of conquistadors fell prisoner to the Aztecs, who claimed the most decisive victory of the siege. After the battle, the Spanish prisoners were sacrificed at the Great Pyramid.

This defeat upset many allied natives who were hoping that Tenochtitlan would have fallen by now. Many of them even returned home since morale in the Spanish camp was slowly falling, but the conquistadors never gave up, despite seeing their fellow crewmates being sacrificed by their enemies. Although the attackers had suffered heavy losses, by late July, they had managed to completely surround the city, achieving their initial goal of cutting it off from the outside.

In the lake, the Aztecs tried to break through the encirclement, but the Spanish ships made sure that no canoes got past. The conquistadors even heavily barricaded the causeways to dissuade the defenders from sallying out. Tenochtitlan was completely isolated, and soon, the toll of the siege started to be felt inside the city.

Already burdened by the plague and lack of manpower, the Aztecs suffered from famine, as they were unable to get food from outside the city. The remaining tributaries that were loyal to the emperor could not get provisions to the capital since allied native patrols controlled the perimeter around the city. Any tribe that sent their forces to aid the Aztecs was ruthlessly met by Spanish guns, something that ensured loyalty from other natives.

Sometime in early August, Cortés was confident that he had suffocated the defenders enough. Tenochtitlan had been completely surrounded for weeks, and the attackers had not launched any new assaults, assuming defensive positions in their camps near the causeways and repelling any attempts of breaking out. Finally, it was time for a push inside the city. Cortés ordered his contingents to attack at the same time from different sides to stretch the defenders' resources. The main attack was concentrated on the northern part of Tenochtitlan, the district of Tlatelolco, which was eventually taken by Alvarado's men. Control of Tlatelolco allowed the conquistadors to push to the city center almost unopposed.

The conquistadors ruthlessly cut their way through the Aztec city and were complemented in their fierceness by their Tlaxcalan allies, who were overzealous to take revenge upon their long-time oppressors. Thousands of Aztecs were slain in the final advance, including many innocent civilians whose homes were looted and ransacked.

Once it was clear that the city had fallen, Cortés tried to contact Emperor Cuauhtémoc to offer the terms of surrender. However, the Aztec *tlatoani* rejected the talks and tried to flee the city with whatever valuables he could take with him. Unfortunately for him, he was caught by Gonzalo de Sandoval and his men and was brought back to Cortés. The news of the captured emperor spread quickly throughout the city, and the remaining Aztec warriors gave up fighting on August 13th, 1521. Cortés brutally tortured Cuauhtémoc, demanding that he return the gold that had been seized from the Spanish during La Noche Trieste, but the emperor and his men swore that they had gotten rid of it already.

The conquistadors had a field day sacking the city in the days following its surrender. They hoarded piles of golden jewelry, coins, and decorations, taking everything that they could to Cortés's quarters, which were set up in the city's main palace. Great Aztec temples were either completely demolished, or their symbols were replaced by Christian imagery. Cuauhtémoc was kept alive. He was still nominally the *tlatoani*, but Cortés had taken charge of the city.

The fall of Tenochtitlan was a crucial event in the history of the Spanish conquest of the Americas. It was, by all means, the first large-scale war between the conquistadors and the natives; all of the previous encounters between them had been small-scale skirmishes. Taking a city of such importance and wealth signaled a great future for Spain in the

New World, and Cortés's fame would skyrocket after word had spread of his successes in Mesoamerica. The campaign against the Aztecs set the stage for decades of brutal conquests, the treatment of the natives by the colonizers, and the subsequent exploitation of their resources. After defeating the biggest and strongest enemy in the region, it became clear that the natives could not really oppose the colonizers.

It is difficult to fully assess the damage that was done during Cortés's two-year campaign since his landing at Veracruz in early 1519. While tens of thousands of natives died as a result of warfare, even more shared the same fate due to the outbreak of smallpox after the conquistadors' initial retreat from the city. Tenochtitlan and many of the surrounding areas fell under the control of the Spanish, and the people who had been subject to Aztec suzerainty for years essentially had new masters.

Cortés would not uphold the concessions he had made to Tlaxcala and other states before his conquest of Tenochtitlan, taking out the potential opposition one by one. With the gold and fame obtained from the destruction of the Aztec Empire, the Spanish conquest of the Americas had begun.

The Defeat of the Purépechans

We have to take into consideration the fact that Hernán Cortés's expedition to what is now modern-day Mexico and his war with the Aztec Empire were not the only ones. Beginning in the early 16th century, there were several simultaneous expeditions directed toward different areas and led and commissioned by different Spaniards. By the time Cortés defeated the Aztecs in the siege of Tenochtitlan in 1521, other explorers had led journeys from Spanish bases of operations in the Caribbean to the North, Central, and South American coasts, with some finding more success than others. Of course, Hernán Cortés will be remembered in history as one of the most iconic conquistadors, not only because he managed to destroy one of the strongest Mesoamerican political entities in the span of two years but also because he was essentially the first one to engage in a drawn-out military conflict in the New World. Cortés was, by all means, the first conquistador, and his brilliant success only promised that there was more for the taking.

The fall of the Aztec Empire was a huge political development in Mesoamerica, as it completely shifted the balance of power in the region. Before 1521, the natives had, more or less, managed to keep the colonizers out of their land, conceding little to them. However, after the fall of Tenochtitlan, it became clear that the Spanish were not messing around. With enough resources and dedication, they had the ability to defeat the natives and take their possessions.

Word quickly spread about the conquistadors' military domination and the horrors of the "great rash" plague, which decimated half of the population of the Aztec capital. No neighboring natives wanted to share the same fate as the Aztecs, so it was only natural that they tried their best to keep the conquistadors at arm's length. Very soon after the fall of Tenochtitlan, Cortés and the conquistadors were approached by messengers from a northern ruler by the name of Tzimtzincha-Tangaxuan II of the Purépecha Empire, which was northeast of Tenochtitlan between the rivers of Lerma and Balsas. The Purépechans, also known as the Tarascans, were based around their capital city of Tzintzuntzan, which was one of the most important ceremonial centers in all of Mesoamerica.

The conquistadors received Tangaxuan II's messengers and accompanied them back to Tzintzuntzan to meet the Purépecha emperor, who was kind enough to offer them gifts in exchange for friendship. However, when the conquistadors presented the gold obtained in Tzintzuntzan to Cortés at Tenochtitlan, the Spanish commander was quick to send an expedition north to take the riches of the city for themselves.

Commanded by Cristóbal de Olid, a portion of the Spanish army arrived at the gates of Tzintzuntzan in 1522. Despite the numerical advantage of the Purépechans, Tangaxuan II chose not to fight the conquistadors. Instead, he peacefully accepted the Spanish as his new suzerains and promised to pay tribute in exchange for retaining his position as ruler. For the next eight years, the Purépechans were in this kind of relationship with the Spanish. It was only in 1530 that the conquistadors conquered Tzintzuntzan and directly came into the possession of the Purépechan lands.

Marquess of the Valley of Oaxaca

As for Cortés himself, he saw Tenochtitlan, which he renamed Mexico City, as his prized possession. Additionally, he dubbed the lands he had conquered from the Aztecs New Spain, signaling a symbolic separation from the Spanish Crown. Mexico City would soon become the base of Spanish colonial operations in the Americas.

To make sure that Mexico was firmly under conquistador rule, the Spanish Crown, then under Holy Roman Emperor and King of Spain Charles V, created the Council of the Indies in 1524 to preside over colonial affairs. Since the Spanish monarch presided over a large territory in Europe, his realm was split into several councils, each of them tasked with the governance of their administrative units, like the Council of Castile, the Council of Flanders, or the Council of Aragon. The councils each had virtually unlimited power when it came to administering their respective regions, and all of them, of course, ultimately answered to the Crown. Thus, it made sense to implement a body with a main focus on colonial affairs in the early days of colonization, especially as the Spanish possessions in the New World were rapidly increasing.

New Spain also saw the establishment of its first royal *audiencia* in 1527, three years after setting up the Council of the Indies. The *audiencias* were essentially regional courts of law that acted as important legal entities. The main goal of the Royal Audiencia of Mexico was to help the council govern New Spain and administer its subjects to make sure they were properly incorporated under Spanish jurisdiction.

King Charles named Cortés the chief justice and governor of New Spain, giving him immense power in the New World, but he also appointed a couple of royal servants to ensure the efficient governance of different administrative branches in the newly conquered lands. This produced a strange relationship between the Spanish Crown and the Viceroyalty of New Spain since it was difficult for the two to maintain close contact due to their remoteness. Essentially, what developed from the very early days of Spanish colonization was a quasi-independent entity in the colonies, which had a large degree of autonomy from the king but also answered to the Crown. The *encomienda* system further reinforced the autonomous nature of New Spain, as the conquistadors transformed into landowners in the newly conquered territories, employing locals to do their bidding.

From the early days since the conquest of the Aztecs, it was clear that New Spain would become the most prosperous Spanish colony. While other colonial activities were going on simultaneously in Central and South America in the 1520s, Cortés's success easily overshadowed every colonial accomplishment in the decade or so immediately after the capture of Tenochtitlan. It was only rivaled by Francisco Pizarro's conquest of the Inca Empire in South America. Cortés would briefly embark on an expedition to Mesoamerica, trying to add more possessions under his belt in what is modern-day Honduras (something we will cover in a later chapter). This expedition, which lasted from 1524 to 1526, did not turn out to be as successful as the conquistador would have hoped, and Cortés returned to Mexico City empty-handed. The conquest of Honduras and the rest of Mesoamerica would take another few decades.

Back in Mexico City, Cortés found his authority challenged by several different figures, who had grown wary of his increasing power and wished to potentially undermine him to gain more for themselves. One of the allegations against Cortés was that he had hidden the income of New Spain from the Crown and had instead used it to enlarge his own *encomienda* and finance more expeditions in Mexico. The Council of the Indies complained about this and other issues before the Spanish Crown, prompting Cortés to sail to Spain to personally deal with the problems.

After Cortés's success, he became a reputable man in the colonies and in Europe and even maintained close contact with King Charles, who appointed him as governor in 1524, sending royal grants to the conquistador through Francisco de Montejo, who had been sent by Cortés during the conquest of the Aztecs to appeal to the Crown. Still, Cortés was forced to return to Spain in 1528 to deal with the allegations, and he had an audience with King Charles to save his reputation.

King Charles had quite a lot on his plate, as he was busy dealing with the ongoing Protestant Reformation and the threat of the Ottoman Empire. He had not been personally involved in colonial affairs, which was one of the reasons behind the introduction of different institutions to preside over colonial matters. He still made time to meet Cortés in person, and the latter was able to successfully defend his case, demonstrating that the charges made against him were untrue. Cortés was proud to tell the king about his achievements and the extension of the Spanish Empire's borders in the New World. His deeds were enough to grab Charles V's attention.

The king further decorated Cortés, giving him the title of marquess of the Valley of Oaxaca, which affirmed his large personal possessions, *encomiendas,* and estates, including the people employed at them. This title was also made hereditary to respect and honor Cortés's achievements, essentially elevating him to a whole new level of prestige.

However, the king decided not to renew Cortés's governorship, preferring instead to assign his own candidate to the position before the introduction of the viceroyalty in 1535. In fact, the decision to make Cortés the marquess was to counterbalance his loss of office, although the conquistador would still retain respect and authority in the colony in the years to come.

All in all, Cortés's return to Spain in 1528 was still a success. He was no longer responsible for managing the colony on an administrative level, meaning that many of his enemies would finally be silenced. Instead, he was granted a massive territory in the heart of Mexico, which basically resulted in him becoming even more wealthy and influential than he had already been. Upon his return to Mexico in 1530, Cortés refrained from getting involved in politics and military expeditions, having already accumulated unparalleled riches and prestige.

The Chichimeca War

Before we move on to how Central America came to be under Spanish rule, we first need to cover how New Spain continued to exist after its establishment as a viceroyalty. New Spain functioned as a sort of a sub-kingdom of Spain, although it was under the control of whoever was the Spanish monarch at the time. Its chief ruler was a royally appointed viceroy who basically had the same control as a king; however, the viceroy was still the subject of the monarch. The position of viceroy was not hereditary, unlike that of a traditional king. We have also already mentioned that *audiencias* were set up to deal with local governance and administration, acting as provincial legal bodies and holding a lot of authority over what transpired in New Spain.

The viceroyalty expanded almost exponentially after the fall of the Aztec Empire. Many surrounding indigenous peoples were already under Spanish control, and many more willingly submitted and joined the *encomienda* in later years. Sometimes, the relationship between the natives and the conquistadors was a bit ambiguous, as had been the case with the Purépechans to the north, who were eventually conquered in 1530. The *encomienda* system and the gradual spread of Christianity in the region made sure that the natives were slowly integrated into a society where the European Spanish stood at the very top of the hierarchy. Over time, the integration efforts would accelerate, and different social classes would emerge in New Spain (as well as in most other Spanish overseas possessions), with the main determinant being the racial and ethnic makeup of a person. Normally, this meant that, for example, the Spaniards born in Europe had more authority and social standing than those born in the New World. Next came those mixed with the indigenous peoples and so on. However, in certain parts of New Spain, the descendants of former noble families of native tribes were respected very much.

Many new cities were founded by the conquistadors in the decades following the fall of the Aztecs, while those destroyed during the campaign, like Tenochtitlan, were rebuilt and remodeled to fit Spanish designs and standards. Some of the most important cities founded by the Spanish include Guadalajara, Puebla de los Ángeles, and Oaxaca City. In the 1530s, the conquistador enterprise expanded, and the various parts of what is modern-day central and southern Mexico were colonized. These new cities attracted more and more people, both from overseas and other Spanish colonies, as well as from the settlements of the indigenous peoples. The cities would grow throughout the centuries to become large population centers in Mexico.

By the 1540s, New Spain's continual growth would be confronted by a challenge in the area known as the Mexican Altiplano—a huge territory occupying the central and northern parts of modern-day Mexico, which is located high above sea level. The Altiplano was not as populated by the conquistadors as other parts of Mexico since it was considered to be an unfriendly place for habitation. Referred to by the Spanish as La Gran Chichimeca, it was mostly inhabited by the indigenous semi-nomadic peoples by the name of the Chichimecas, who mainly survived through hunting and gathering.

The Chichimecas constantly moved around the plain to find suitable places for food and dwelling. They were far less advanced than the Aztecs. They did not have large urban centers like the people from the southern parts of Mexico and the rest of Mesoamerica. The mountainous region in which the Chichimecas were situated provided them with a natural barrier of defense from the other indigenous tribes, and they largely developed separately from the more advanced civilizations of Mexico, having more in common with those indigenous groups who lived in the modern-day US.

By the time the Spanish arrived in the region, the Chichimecan political organization was that of a confederation of various tribes, the largest of which were the Guachichiles, the Guamares, the Pames, and the Zacatecas. Although these tribes mostly lived in peace, they were, nevertheless, fierce warriors with advanced tactics and weapons. The Spanish noted their proficiency with bows and their usage of obsidian in arrowheads, which made the arrows very sharp. Their arrows were able to penetrate the heavy armor of the conquistadors.

The first real encounter between the Spanish and the Chichimecas was during the Mixtón War—a name given to a conflict that was started by the rebellious indigenous Caxcan people in northwestern Mexico in the year 1540. The Caxcanes were also semi-nomads but relied more on agriculture than hunting and gathering. They were ruthlessly conquered by the conquistadors after the fall of the Aztec Empire. The Spanish finally won over them in the late 1520s and early 1530s, using many of their Mexican allies in the battles and imposing a harsh rule upon the Caxcanes due to their resistance.

However, in the year 1540, the Caxcanes rebelled against New Spain, prompting Viceroy Antonio de Mendoza to send for help to Pedro de Alvarado, a conquistador who is best remembered for his role in the conquest of a large part of Central America. The Caxcanes were aided by the Chichimeca people, and they achieved initial success against the conquistadors, pushing into the Spanish city of Guadalajara in 1541.

After being unable to deal with the rebels in the first phase of the war, Mendoza assembled a huge army consisting of at least thirty thousand conquered Mexican natives and marched to the natives' position in the north. Eventually, in early 1542, the conquistador-Mexican forces took Mixtón, the Caxcanes' main base of operations, ending the rebellion. The Spanish harshly punished those who had resisted. Still, the war against the northern peoples of Mexico proved to be quite a challenge for Mendoza, and the Spanish noted the military prowess of the Chichimecas throughout their skirmishes in the war.

Despite regaining control of the Caxcanes, the conquistadors largely stayed out of La Gran Chichimeca after the Mixtón War, with only minor settlements established in the area. However, in 1546, reports spread from one of the Spanish settlements in the north about the discovery of silver, prompting a renewed interest in the region and the migration of many Spaniards to the newly founded Spanish town at Bufa Hill, which would eventually become the modern city of Zacatecas. The word of silver seemed to be true, as the conquistadors established several mines throughout the area with the hopes of setting up a good connection between the region and the cities in the south.

The migrants disregarded the indigenous Chichimecas and disturbed their way of life. It became obvious that the nomads could not peacefully coexist with the conquistadors in the Altiplano without compromising a lot. While the conquistadors tried to subjugate the Chichimecas and use them as slaves to work in their new mines, the natives responded by coming together, ambushing Spanish trade caravans and launching raids on the conquistador towns. These developments started a long and drawn-out conflict between the conquistadors and the Chichimeca peoples, which would persist for several decades and be very costly for both sides.

The hostilities began to break out in the early 1550s when the natives launched a couple of preemptive strikes on the conquistadors. The Chichimeca were well aware of their surroundings and utilized their numerical advantage, attacking quickly and effectively. They took out whole bands of Spanish before looting them and retreating. The conquistadors could do little to stop the natives' attacks, and by 1555, the Chichimeca skirmishes were becoming quite a detriment to the cohesiveness of the mining and trading operations in the Altiplano.

The Spanish wagons needed to undergo a long and tenuous journey from Zacatecas, where the mined silver was accumulated, to Mexico City and other areas under conquistador control. The raids on the passing caravans dealt serious blows to the colonizers, who not only lost a substantial amount of money but also suffered thousands of casualties, with the Chichimeca claiming the lives of conquistadors and their allied natives. The dangers posed by the hostile groups isolated Zacatecas from the rest of the colony, and any traveler or trader who was able to complete the journey through the unsafe lands was greatly respected by the Spanish, driving up the prices of silver and regular goods in Zacatecas.

At first, the Spanish response was incohesive since the conquistador activity in the region was largely private, with independent groups of Spaniards having ventured to Zacatecas during the silver rush. Initially, the consensus was that these daring individuals knew what they were getting into, going deep into unconquered territories, away from the safety of the conquistadors' holdings in the south. But as the government of New Spain became more and more interested in mining the silver available in the central and northern parts of the Mexican Altiplano, it started sending its own men, investing a lot of resources in the expeditions to Zacatecas and back.

The main goal was to establish a relatively secure route, but the threat of the Chichimeca made it extremely difficult. The officials of the viceroyalty saw the terrible effects of the Chichimeca attacks and decided to change their approach, adopting a new policy in the 1560s that would send more armed forces to the region to deal with the troublesome natives and defend the trade caravans.

One way to implement this strategy was to set up small forts along the main route to Zacatecas and the mining settlements of the Altiplano, with the main fortification being established at San Felipe. While bands of conquistadors and allied Mexican natives were stationed along the way, the government urged the population to migrate to the north, thinking that with more people, the settlements would hold out better. Although this was theoretically a good strategy, not a lot of people chose to move to Zacatecas since it was hard for them to abandon their already established homes in the south in favor of the unknown. Those who did go generally met the same gruesome fate at the hands of the Chichimeca.

These initiatives did not result in any advantage for the Spanish, as the Chichimeca responded by continuing their raids on a larger and more organized scale. Hundreds of conquistadors and native inhabitants of New Spain died every week at the hands of the natives, and a sense of safety never developed in the northern Spanish settlements. The conquistadors tried to confront the Chichimeca forces head-on, but the latter always managed to choose fights they knew they could win. The manpower the confederation possessed was enough for them to emerge victorious continuously throughout the 1570s and the early 1580s, making it the first time that the conquistadors had failed to quell the native resistance in the Americas throughout the course of multiple decades. Finally, the conquistadors started to realize that constantly fighting in unfavorable conditions in the home of the Chichimeca was foolish. The natives had a natural advantage. They knew the area better and were free to act whenever they wished. After decades of inconsequential fighting, a larger part of the population started protesting to make it stop.

The main voices for making peace with the Chichimecas were found in the Christian communities and missionaries of New Spain. Beginning in the late 1570s, they protested in favor of ending the conflict, noting that the conquistadors who had taken over Chichimeca land in the north were provoking the natives by enslaving and killing members of their tribes. This assertion was largely true; when the Spanish arrived in the silver-rich areas of the Altiplano, they needed more people to do the difficult work of mining and were very quick to start attacking the natives to forcefully employ them in the mines. Since the war with the Chichimeca had cost New Spain a lot of money and men with no successful outcome, the newly appointed viceroy Álvaro Manrique de Zúñiga was convinced in 1586 to appeal to those who urged making peace.

Instead of an aggressive, militaristic response to Chichimeca aggression, a peaceful and gradual approach was proposed. No more military expeditions would be allowed in the area in order to prevent the situation from escalating yet again. To achieve peace, the conquistadors approached Chichimeca leaders with gifts, such as clothing and weapons, and these overtures were quite successful. The nomadic tribes would be pacified as long as the Spanish activity did not interfere with their own in the region, and they demanded the release of prisoners, a demand that was accepted by the conquistadors. In addition, the viceroy, after consulting with the clergy, decided to gradually establish more small towns in La Gran Chichimeca, which would serve as the next steps of pacification. The idea was to gradually convert the Chichimeca to Christianity.

The slow approach worked, as hostilities ended in the following years. The royal road from Mexico City to Zacatecas became safer. This, in turn, accelerated Spanish and native migration to the region, and the emergence of new, agrarian settlements and towns slowly had the desired effect of assimilating the Chichimeca. At first, the nomads were provided with essential resources to establish friendly relations, but the continuously peaceful cultural and social exchange made the Chichimeca transform the makeup of their tribes and slowly become integrated into New Spain.

Still, the conflict between the conquistadors and the Chichimeca still remains one of the rare examples of colonial wars that saw the natives defeating the colonizers. This occurrence was significant since it demonstrated that a cohesive effort could have been made by the natives to resist colonization and emerge victorious, even though the Chichimeca did become subjects in the end. Just military prowess and victories in battles were not enough to quell the native resistance. Before reverting to completely different methods, the Spanish had been losing for multiple decades against the confederation of semi-nomadic tribes in the Mexican Altiplano.

Once a secure link between Mexico City and Zacatecas was established, New Spain had an avenue to further expand its activities in the northern parts of Mexico, and the silver mines generated a huge source of income for the viceroyalty. Spanish colonization in North America continued, and New Spain would eventually grow to become one of the largest colonial entities in history. Still, the Chichimeca War was one of the last large-scale conflicts in the region between the conquistadors and the natives. While it was underway, equally interesting developments were unfolding in other parts of the New World.

Chapter Four – Spain in Mesoamerica

Trouble in Honduras

By 1524, Cortés had consolidated his position in the former Aztec territories. He had led the effort to rebuild Tenochtitlan and transform the city spiritually, allowing the natives to be familiarized with Catholicism. The *encomiendas* ensured economic stability, and the conquistadors managed to set up reliable trade routes to the eastern coast, further connecting Mexico City to the Spanish possessions in the Caribbean. The small delegation Cortés had sent to Iberia to represent him before the Crown had been successful, returning to the conquistador after the capture of Tenochtitlan and bringing royal grants from the king. Charles V's court was impressed by Cortés's achievements, so they also issued him an official coat of arms, greatly increasing his prestige.

Cortés's rival, Governor Velázquez of Cuba, passed away in 1524, ending the hostilities between the Caribbean colonies and the conquistador and allowing him more freedom to pursue the conquest of the rest of Mesoamerica. With the Purépecha Empire already subjugated in the north, Cortés wished to turn his attention to the southeast and try to better explore the Yucatán Peninsula and its surrounding areas, where the locals were nearly as rich as the Aztecs had been.

Although the Yucatán was a hot commodity in the early 1520s, more and more conquistador expeditions were taking place to its south in today's Central America, exploring modern-day Honduras, Nicaragua, Belize, and Guatemala by the time Cortés ordered Cristóbal de Olid to march down there. These expeditions, which had arrived in Central America at different times, all had claims on different portions of land they had colonized, eventually coming into conflict with each other.

Firstly, there was Gil González Dávila and his expedition, which had set out from Santo Domingo in early 1524 and landed on the northern coast of modern-day Honduras. There, they founded a town by the name of Puerto de Ceballos. He then divided up his men and explored the south and west, trying to reach the Pacific Ocean. In the Olancho Valley, Dávila's men came across other conquistadors from the expedition led by Hernando de Soto, but instead of getting on friendly terms with each other, the two conquistador forces engaged in a battle, trying to claim the unexplored lands for themselves. Francisco Hernández de Córdoba also led an expedition in the Yucatán, complicating matters even more.

Recognizing that the region was up for grabs, Cortés, who was already regarded as the most accomplished conquistador, did not want to miss out. He sent Cristóbal de Olid with a decent-sized force to claim the contested lands for him in January 1524. After the latter briefly resupplied in Santo Domingo, he landed east of Puerto de Ceballos—the settlement founded by González Dávila—at Triunfo de la Cruz. But after initially claiming the land in the name of Cortés, he changed his mind and declared himself as the ruler, defying his orders. Just like that, another contestant was added to the scramble.

When word of Olid's rebellion reached Cortés in Mexico City, he sent another expedition, this time under his cousin, Francisco de las Casas, to bring the rebels back under his control, but las Casas's men would be eventually defeated by Olid and taken prisoner. Cristóbal de Olid managed to withstand the pressure from Cortés and other conquistadors in the region and emerged as a dominant force in Honduras in the early fall of 1524.

Cortés finally took matters into his own hands. In October 1524, he personally led an overland expedition to Honduras to subdue the rebellious Cristóbal de Olid. He marched south from Mexico City with an army of about two hundred conquistadors and a couple of thousand local Mexicans, as well as the Aztec Emperor Cuauhtémoc, who was still his prisoner. Cortés crossed the southwestern parts of the Yucatán Peninsula through modern-day Petén, Guatemala. There, he encountered the Itzá people of Maya ethnicity, who actually received the conquistadors with friendship and gifts. They allowed Cortés to visit their cities if the main army remained outside. Cortés was impressed by the cities' complexity and interconnectedness, noting their easily defendable locations (they were situated in a mountainous region). Upon their visit to the island city of Nojtepén in Lake Petén Itzá, King Kan Ek' of the Itzá greeted Cortés very enthusiastically and even let the conquistadors set up a Christian cross in the city for his own worship.

Still, despite friendly encounters with the natives, Cortés and his expedition were plagued by unfavorable travel conditions. Crossing the Maya Mountains proved to be an especially difficult task, causing the deaths of many conquistadors and horses. The conquistadors also had logistical difficulties. When they left the Itzá Kingdom, they entered remote hilly areas where it was difficult to get provisions. After weeks of struggling, the expedition finally made its way to Amatique Bay. The much friendlier natural conditions allowed the conquistadors to regroup and continue their march to the east.

To his disappointment (and relief), Cortés and his weakened force would not be necessary to deal with the rebels by the time of their arrival in Honduras. Although Cristóbal de Olid initially managed to imprison other conquistadors with rival claims, he became a victim of a mutiny. Francisco de las Calas and Gil González Dávila managed to break free from their imprisonment, capturing Olid and sentencing him to death in a trial. Las Casas then declared himself to be the new governor of Honduras before founding the city of Trujillo and then sailing off to Mexico.

In mid-1525, Cortés finally arrived in Honduras by sea and was greeted by men who were no longer hostile toward him. Since Cortés was the one who had originally sent las Casas to govern in his name, he assumed the leadership of the colony and ordered the conquistadors to explore the area to get a better understanding of it. In the following months, the conquistadors managed to expand their reach to the south, linking their possessions in Honduras to Nicaragua. Before leaving for Mexico in April 1526, Cortés essentially controlled the northern part of Honduras, while the rest of Central America was still disputed between several different conquistadors.

Montejo in the Yucatán

The Yucatán Peninsula, as we have already mentioned, held a lot of interest for the conquistadors. However, the early expeditions provided the Spanish with little avenues, as they only managed to explore the shores of the peninsula, being unable to progress farther inland. Later on, Cortés chose to ignore the heart of the peninsula, circling Yucatán to get to the Aztec lands in the heart of Mexico. When the conquistador set out to quell the rebellion in Honduras, he did not engage in military activities with the native peoples on a scale similar to what he had done with the Aztecs.

Still, the territory remained largely unexplored and uncolonized, so it was only natural for the conquistadors to direct their attention to it, especially since it served as a corridor between Cortés's New Spain and the newly established colonies in Central America. They were also aware of the prosperity of the Maya and their riches. In the late 1520s, the first efforts to actually conquer the Yucatán were made.

The conquistador who is largely responsible for shifting the attention of the colonizers to the peninsula is Francisco de Montejo. He was a veteran explorer and a close friend of Cortés; we have already mentioned him above in connection to his role as the latter's dignitary to the Spanish Crown. Upon his return to New Spain in 1522, he brought royal grants and privileges for Cortés, but he had to travel back to Europe a couple of years later to defend Cortés once again in front of the royal court. The conqueror of the Aztecs and the future viceroy of New Spain was accused of abusing his power in the colonies and acting on his own instead of being reliant on royal orders. Montejo was once again successful in defending him in the years between 1524 and 1525, earning great respect and sympathy for his actions in the eyes of the Crown.

The Crown not only named Montejo an *adelantado* and gave him his own coat of arms, two decisions that proved his status, but also granted him the right to colonize and claim the lands of the Yucatán Peninsula for Spain, commissioning an official royal expedition. This meant that Montejo, who was already quite rich from his travels and *encomiendas*, had the opportunity to expand his prestige and finally come into possession of the missing link between New Spain and Honduras.

In early 1527, Francisco de Montejo left Spain with a sizeable force of four hundred men and four ships, plus supplies and military equipment.

After an initial pit stop in Santo Domingo, his expedition landed at the island of Cozumel, already a known location for the Spanish conquistadors. After being received there by the locals, the expedition then progressed west, reaching the Maya province of Ekab on the eastern coast of the Yucatán. The conquistadors proceeded to take the town of Xel-ha from the natives, who stood no chance against the Spanish guns. While some natives stayed in the town and were forced to work under the conquistadors, many chose to flee to the west, to the safety of the peninsula's Maya heartland.

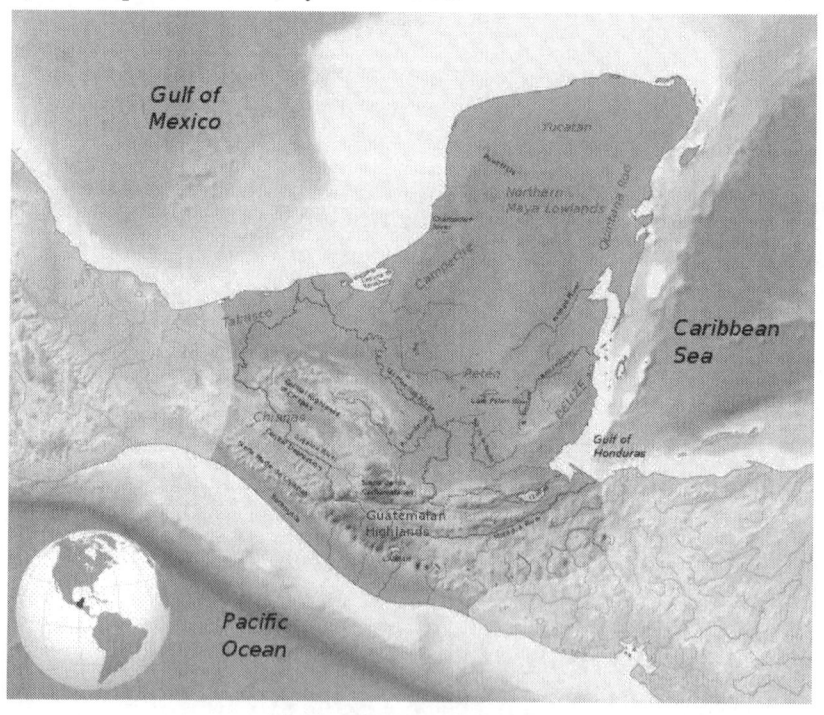

A look at the Maya civilization.
Simon Burchell, CC BY-SA 4.0 <https://creativecommons.org/licenses/by-sa/4.0>, via Wikimedia Commons; https://commons.wikimedia.org/wiki/File:Maya_civilization_location_map_-_geography.svg

After making a brief stop at Xel-ha, the conquistadors made their way north along the coast. By the end of 1527, Montejo's expedition reached the northern tip of Yucatán, encountering several small Maya towns and forcing the natives to declare their loyalty. By the beginning of 1528, the Spanish had claimed the eastern coast of the Yucatán Peninsula without much resistance. They never quite engaged with the locals on a large scale in the province of Ekab, so they never did do much conquering per se. Montejo's expedition seemed to be more like the ones before

Cortés's conquest of Tenochtitlan; it was chiefly for exploration and the establishment of contacts in the peninsula.

In the spring of 1528, Montejo and his men continued their journey to the province of Chikinchel, located in the northern part of the Yucatán, making their way to the city of Chauaca, which they found to be abandoned by the locals. In Chikinchel, the conquistadors encountered various forms of resistance from the locals, having to fight their way through a couple of ambushes before eventually engaging in a large-scale skirmish with the locals at the city of Ake, near modern-day Mérida, Mexico. The conquistadors were able to defeat the Maya every time but sustained heavy casualties after the continuous attacks of the natives.

Thus, after the victory at Ake, Montejo chose not to continue the expedition, turning back with whatever men he had left to the town of Xel-ha, where he had left a small garrison. However, once they made their way back, the Spanish found the garrisons of the towns they had taken on the eastern coast of the peninsula to have been almost completely wiped out. It seemed that once the main force was gone and had taken most of the equipment with it, the natives had organized several attacks on the conquistador-controlled towns. The Spanish at Xel-ha had barely managed to hold on and were reassured with the return of Montejo and the rest of the expedition.

Due to the casualties they had sustained, the conquistadors considered giving up whatever they had gained in the Yucatán and leaving the peninsula, but their enthusiasm was reignited when a support ship arrived from Santo Domingo with more men and supplies. Montejo had planned the arrival of reinforcements ahead of arriving in the Yucatán when he had made a stop in Cuba at the beginning of his journey. Because of these reinforcements, Montejo decided to explore south along the coast of the peninsula, marching down to the town of Chetumal, some 160 miles or so south of Xel-ha.

After a long and strenuous journey, he would stumble upon Gonzalo Guerrero, the shipwrecked Spaniard who still lived among the natives after ending up there in 1511. Just like Cortés, Montejo asked him to join his expedition, but Guerrero politely declined and remained with the tribe.

Weary of the Maya, the conquistadors refrained from going deep into the peninsula and stuck to the shore to avoid any ambushes and skirmishes with the natives. Eventually, Montejo and his men passed along the eastern coast of the Yucatán, ending up in the northwestern part of Honduras, where the Ulúa River links up with the Caribbean, before deciding to turn back.

Thus, Montejo's initial campaign to conquer the Yucatán was not as successful as the conquistador would have hoped. The peninsula still remained a rather mysterious place to the Spanish, who had been unable to bring the Maya people of the area under their control. Whatever towns the Spanish had founded and controlled were all along the coast, but they were heavily disconnected from each other by the year 1530; by that point, other conquistadors were finding much more success in the rest of the New World. The Yucatán was necessary for an overland link between the colonies of New Spain and Honduras, but its dangerous lowlands and the determination of the people who inhabited it made it extremely difficult for the Spanish to get a firm grip over the peninsula.

Unlike Mexico, which was essentially fully controlled by the Aztec Empire and its tributaries, the Maya civilization of Yucatán was far less centralized. This meant that making progress against one tribe or city-state in the area did not necessarily translate into progress when it came to others. The Maya were better prepared to answer the aggression of the conquistadors with their own aggression, employing guerrilla tactics, setting up ambushes, and cutting off the conquistador troops whenever they had the opportunity. Different towns were eventually captured by the Spanish, but since the Yucatán did not have a central administrative capital like Tenochtitlan, the loss of these towns was not considered to have been the end of the world for the natives. In the Yucatán, the conquistadors had to work very hard to quell the Maya, and it would take them more than a decade after Montejo's initial campaign to fully come into possession of the peninsula.

Conquest of the Maya

Efforts to take the Yucatán continued throughout the 1530s, and this time, it would be Francisco de Montejo the Younger who would help take control of the peninsula. Francisco de Montejo the Elder had left for Mexico in 1528, halting the expedition in the Yucatán for a little bit and entrusting the command of the remaining troops to Alonso de Ávila, who had beforehand been the leader of the garrison at Xel-ha.

While Montejo was busy being named the governor of the province of Tabasco of New Spain and struggling to fight against the natives and the rebellious conquistadors there, little went on when it came to completing the conquest of the Yucatán. Ávila recognized the compromised position of Xel-ha and abandoned the settlement to move the headquarters a bit north to Xelanca, which was still on the eastern coast of the Yucatán, before eventually setting up a new base on the northern coast of the peninsula at Champoton.

By 1530, the conquistadors had completely abandoned their starting position on the eastern side of the peninsula and had to recalibrate their strategy in terms of how to approach the Maya who inhabited the area. From their previous experiences, the Spanish were aware of the Maya fighting spirit and tactics. They realized they needed to conduct a large campaign against the natives to avoid further complications and finally conquer the peninsula.

In 1531, Montejo once again resumed the efforts to conquer the Yucatán, this time with the help of his son and Ávila, who had accumulated a lot of knowledge about the area. The expedition began in Campeche, located on the southwestern coast of the peninsula, and planned to first go northeast and then south to consolidate Spanish control. However, with the resources the conquistadors had at their disposal, it was virtually impossible to take firm control of the Yucatán, but the Spaniards were nevertheless determined to try.

Before they could embark on a campaign, the Spanish settlement at Campeche was attacked by a large native army, but the conquistadors were able to defend their position, driving the Maya back with the might of their guns and crossbows. The encounter at Campeche made it clear that the Maya stood no chance in a head-to-head battle. The Maya had neither the manpower nor the military capabilities of the Aztecs to put up a serious fight. The only way the conquistadors could lose was to become outmaneuvered by the natives and take unfavorable fights.

The Montejos and Ávila launched a series of campaigns into the northern part of the Yucatán to deal with independent Maya kingdoms and confederations in late 1531. Their attention was mainly focused on the chiefdom of Cupul (Kupul) in the central part of the peninsula. Cupul was one of the largest and most important Maya provinces, with its capital of Chichén Itzá, a magnificent city containing diverse architectural styles, great pyramids, and ritualistic centers. The different Maya chiefdoms had popped up in the area after the collapse of a larger empire in the Yucatán. The turbulent social and political developments significantly weakened the Maya civilization, which had existed and prospered for thousands of years before the arrival of the Spanish.

In fact, before Spanish colonization, the Maya reached the peak of their power, but constant wars, famines, and diseases contributed to the decline of the civilization and the separation of the people into different chiefdoms (*kuchkabals*) by the mid-15th century. Since many great cities were abandoned and population centers moved from one place to another in the Yucatán, the Maya were not ready to put up a good fight, but they still successfully managed to upset many of the Spanish efforts to subjugate them.

The conquistadors managed to get to Chichén Itzá without much resistance, and the chief of Cupul allowed them to settle the lands near the city. Francisco de Montejo the Younger was content with this development and divided up the lands entrusted to him by the locals between his men, creating *encomiendas* in the province. Chichén Itzá was not as rich or populous as Tenochtitlan, but it was still a very important religious center for the natives.

However, the conquistadors overstayed their welcome, as the native population was soon upset by the presence of the Spaniards and their treatment of the indigenous people. About half a year after the arrival of the Spanish, the locals revolted against the conquistadors, forcing them to rush into the city to defend themselves against armed natives. In the skirmishes that broke out, the chief of Cupul was killed, and Francisco de Montejo the Younger just managed to survive. With his forces badly damaged, he held out in Chichén Itzá until mid-1533 but then decided to retreat to the western province of Ah Kin Chel. There, he was received by natives who were more loyal to the Spanish. He eventually regrouped with his father in the city of Mani, southwest of Chichén Itzá.

During this time, Francisco de Montejo the Elder had split his forces and taken them to Mani in the Maya *kuchkabal* controlled by the Xiu family. Here, Montejo managed to get on friendlier terms with the natives, founding a couple of Spanish towns but not achieving anything significant. Even after uniting with his son, the combined conquistador army was unable to progress much farther into the Yucatán. The relative inactivity and the lack of progress in the campaign, as well as an insignificant amount of loot, made many colonizers leave for Mexico or the Caribbean to try their luck elsewhere. It was a logical decision. Montejo had actively tried to take control of the peninsula and defeat the Maya since 1527, but for more than seven years, his efforts had not amounted to anything. The Spaniards gradually started their retreat from Mani to Campeche and then to Veracruz in 1534, abandoning their possessions in the area and not returning to the Yucatán for the next few years.

Francisco de Montejo the Younger would launch another offensive in the Yucatán Peninsula in 1540. The objective, once again, was the conquest of the Maya peoples in the northern and central parts of the Yucatán. By this time, other Spanish conquistadors were far more successful in defeating the Maya in other parts of Central America, most importantly in the highlands of Guatemala and Honduras. The Yucatán's lowlands essentially remained the only location where the conquistadors were unable to assert their dominance.

Montejo launched his expedition from Champoton and moved toward Campeche with about four or five hundred men, all armed to the teeth and determined to finally subjugate the Maya. The campaign set out in 1541 and seemed to be more promising, as the conquistadors progressed successfully past the locals. In early 1542, the colonizers founded the town of Mérida in the northwestern part of the peninsula, which would eventually become the largest in the Yucatán. There, they set up a council and their headquarters. They also managed to convince many of the locals to peacefully accept them as their new suzerains and convert to Christianity.

The head of the powerful Xiu family, which was centered around the city of Mani and had been friendly toward the conquistadors before, was one of the first to accept Christianity. He was baptized and stayed with the Spanish for a couple of months out of his own interest. According to the records, he was impressed by the Catholic faith and greatly respected the colonizers. Thanks to his conversion, many of the neighboring Maya lords were also convinced to get on friendly terms with the conquistadors instead of being hostile toward them. Thus, by mid-1542, much of the western part of the peninsula was at least nominally under Spanish rule. The Spanish received supplies, provisions, and gifts from various Maya chiefs. Chichén Itzá and the eastern Maya chiefdoms still had to be conquered.

The eastern independent chiefdoms posed more of a threat to Montejo, and the organized resistance dragged out the conquistador campaign for more than three additional years. The *kuchkabals* of Cupul, Chetumel, Ekab, Chikinchel, Uaymil, and Tazes all proved to be a thorn in the side of the Spanish, who were constantly forced to confront the natives in unfavorable battlefields in the Yucatán lowlands. Surrounded by dense forests and foliage, the Maya were relentless, constantly ambushing the conquistadors and only taking the fights they knew they would win. By late 1544, Montejo and his men had made several attempts to fully conquer the people of these provinces, and although they did occasionally take some settlements, they never truly established a firm grip on this side of the peninsula until late 1546 after receiving numerous reinforcements.

In fact, the Maya *kuchkabals* had united against their common enemy for the first time after the collapse of the larger kingdoms and the emergence of decentralized chiefdoms, but the technological and strategic disparities between them and the Spanish proved to be too much to overcome, leaving them powerless in the end. Most of the important Maya cities were captured by the conquistadors by early 1547. Francisco de Montejo the Younger (alongside his father, who rejoined the conquistador campaign despite the fact that he was in his late sixties) finally came to control most of the Yucatán.

Although 1546 is considered to be the year when the Maya in the Yucatán Peninsula were defeated, it was by no means the end of the struggle between the natives and the colonizers in the region. Thousands abandoned their homes and fled to the south, reaching Lake Petén, where Hernán Cortés had been received in 1525 on his way to Honduras. There, the Maya would last for another hundred or so years until the conquistadors launched a series of concentrated offensives against the Itzá Kingdom in the region. But before then, the conquest of the Yucatán was completed at great cost to the colonizers.

Pedro de Alvarado in Guatemala

Parallel to the expeditions in Yucatán, the Spanish were also active in other parts of Central America. For the conquistadors, getting to previously unknown places and colonizing them was a priority since it would guarantee them rights to the riches and lands they would conquer. In most cases, personal glory and enrichment drove the conquistadors, not a higher motive of enlightening the people they came across and bringing "civilization" to them, as many colonizers would later claim. Many conquistadors flocked to the lands of Central America, landing at different points and succeeding, in various degrees, at colonizing different strips of land.

Central America was an especially hot commodity after the conquest of the Aztec Empire by Cortés. After the fall of Tenochtitlan, few expeditions were directed toward the exploration of Mexico, as it had already been claimed by and governed by Cortés. Challenging him over the control of the lands he had spent years to conquer seemed foolish. However, the Central American strip (the part between Mexico and South America), which the conquistadors knew was not that large and contained gold, promised to be a suitable destination for any newcomer who wished to take it. Still, even in this area, conquests would be modeled after Cortés's expedition, and the conquistadors who led the campaigns against the native population would mostly be those who had already served with Cortés and gotten a lot of experience.

Francisco de Montejo, a trusted friend of Cortés, is one of the examples. Of course, it would take him (and his son) more than twenty years to conquer the northern part of the Yucatán. Additionally, with the prestige he had obtained thanks to his successful interactions with the royal court, Montejo was considered an accomplished person when he embarked on the first of his many efforts against the Maya of the Yucatán in the late 1520s. Cristóbal de Olid, the self-declared ruler of Honduras, had also been sent by Cortés to take control of the south in his name. He rebelled and was eventually killed in a mutiny, but the person who replaced him, Francisco de las Casas, was also a trusted friend of Cortés. Later on, several conquistadors would compete for domination in this part of Central America.

Another conquistador who had served with Cortés and later played a big role in the conquest of Central America was Pedro de Alvarado, who was famous (or infamous) for his role during the massacre at the Great Pyramid in Tenochtitlan in 1520. Later on, he participated in the conquest of the Aztec capital and was rewarded greatly by Cortés for his efforts. About a year after the conquest of Tenochtitlan, Alvarado was dispatched south with a sizeable conquistador force and thousands of allied Mexican natives. The reason behind this expedition was the same as it had been in other cases: the subjugation of the native peoples in what is today Guatemala.

After the fall of Tenochtitlan, Cortés and the conquistadors were approached by different tribes that tried to appeal to the Spanish in order not to meet the same fate as the Aztecs. Like the Purépechans from the north, who chose not to fight against the conquistadors and willingly agreed to pay tribute to avoid bloodshed, the conquistadors received messengers from the Maya in the southern Guatemalan Highlands as early as 1522.

This area was densely inhabited by the Maya, much like the Yucatán Peninsula, but unlike the Yucatán, it was an uneven, mountainous region with many rivers and a similar decentralized political structure. Several different indigenous Maya peoples inhabited the area, each with their own separate languages.

Cortés was approached by the K'iche', who were centered around the city of Q'umarkaj, and the Kaqchikel peoples from the city of Iximche. These messengers willingly submitted to the rule of Cortés and invited the conquistadors to their cities as a sign of friendship. Although the exact details of what happened next are unknown, Cortés did send a small mission to Guatemala to meet with the rulers of the natives. However, instead of peacefully approaching the Maya in the highlands, the conquistador ordered Pedro de Alvarado to assemble a force and launch an offensive to subjugate them. The reason behind this is unknown. Either the returning Spanish reported that the natives were not actually loyal and wanted to take advantage of the conquistadors, or they became aware of the gold in the mountains of Guatemala. In any case, Alvarado was more than happy to march south, embarking on a campaign in 1523 that would eventually result in the Spanish conquest of a significant portion of Mesoamerica.

The Sierra Madre Mountains, which were inhabited by the Maya, provided them with a natural defensive barrier against the Spanish, but the conquistadors would still be able to get the upper hand relatively easily from the very beginning. Marching down south along the coast of the Pacific from Mexico City, Alvarado and his men eventually ended up at the Samala River, and after some skirmishes, they were able to make their way over the river into the K'iche' Kingdom. Since this region was densely populated, they encountered many small settlements on their way to the main city of Q'umarkaj, the ruins of which still survive today.

By early 1524, the expedition had defeated the K'iche' army at Zapotitlán, sacking the town and proceeding along the river. As the Spanish force made its way to Quetzaltenango, it had to defend itself from the many K'iche' ambushes along the way, emerging victorious thanks to their cavalry and guns. The natives had never encountered such technology, let alone horses, and were thus gradually driven back. By mid-February 1524, they put up a final stand, where they were crushed by Alvarado's men. Out of about thirty thousand natives, more than half were slain on the battlefield, while the rest were forced to flee or were captured. After the battle, the surviving K'iche' lords and nobles surrendered to the conquistadors, opening the way to Q'umarkaj.

However, Alvarado was wary of the natives. He knew of their tactics and their tendency to go back on their word, so after entering the city without resistance, he set up his camp outside of it and invited the K'iche' rulers to discuss the terms of surrender. The king of the K'iche' and his companions arrived at Alvarado's camp to declare fealty to the Spaniards, but the latter decided to imprison the king to dissuade his men from attacking the conquistadors. Then, he ordered his soldiers to loot the city and burned Q'umarkaj down, once again earning himself notoriety.

By March 1524, after the K'iche' capital was reduced to ashes, Alvarado decided to make contact with the Kaqchikel people of the city of Iximche. It appears the Kaqchikel emerged as allies to the Spanish after hearing of the fate of the K'iche'. They invited the conquistadors to their capital and cordially received them. Then, they offered assistance against the remaining natives who were still hostile toward the Spanish, sending hundreds of men to join Alvarado's force, which now included not only the Mexican natives but also the Maya. Alvarado was satisfied by the submission of the natives, and he claimed Iximche for himself, declaring it the capital of a new colony in Central America in July 1524. Iximche was the local Maya name of the city; in Nahuatl (which was used by the natives in the Spanish army and, therefore, by the Spanish themselves), it was referred to as the "land of the forests" or Guatemala. Alvarado thus dubbed the city and the new colony Guatemala and then proceeded to extend its borders beyond what the Kaqchikel had controlled.

During his stay in Iximche, Alvarado took his men, along with the new Kaqchikel allies, to the west near Lake Atitlán to fight the Tz'utujil, who were situated around the lake's basin. The natives surrendered without putting up much resistance. After the conquistadors captured their capital city of Tecpán Atitlán, the Tz'utujil sent their chiefs to Alvarado, who pledged loyalty to the Spanish. The Tz'utujil lords were followed by representatives of many neighboring cities, who brought gifts and wished to ally themselves with the Spanish. They believed it was better to accept their rule than try to fight them off. By the autumn of 1524, the conquistadors had established control over a large portion of the Guatemalan Highlands, but the main fight was still to be fought.

Alvarado shifted his attention to the rest of the people in the area. Having captured most of the Guatemalan Highlands, he now wished to take the fight to the Pacific coast, which was mostly inhabited by the Xinca and the Pipil. They were very different from other natives in Mesoamerica. They spoke completely different languages and lived largely in isolation from the Maya, who dominated the Yucatán and most of Guatemala. Some accounts suggest that Alvarado's decision to campaign against the Pipil at Izcuintepeque stemmed from the fact that the latter was at war with the Kaqchikel, who may have persuaded the conquistador to take his men to defeat them.

In any case, after the victory against the Tz'utujil, Alvarado and a sizeable force of a couple of thousand men launched a brutal campaign against the natives. The Pipil and the Xinca settlements fell one by one. It is difficult to estimate how many natives died in combat. By the end of the year, the conquistadors had ravaged the Pacific Lowlands and had subjugated its population.

The relationship between the conquistadors and their Kaqchikel allies would soon deteriorate, as the Spanish were despised not only because they were foreign intruders but also because they did not show much respect and honor in their interactions with the natives. The Spanish soldiers were each assigned *encomiendas* by Alvarado, and the natives were overwhelmed with the work their Spanish masters assigned them. In addition, Alvarado imposed a very large tribute on the lords of Iximche, essentially rebuking the acceptance the natives had shown the colonizers. Continued confrontations between the conquistadors and the locals eventually strained the relationship beyond repair. After an incident where the Spanish burned down a holy site in the city, the Kaqchikel decided to rise up.

In mid-1526, the hostile natives drove the conquistadors out of Guatemala City, forcing them to relocate to the west and regroup before striking back. This coincided with the end of Hernán Cortés's expedition to Honduras, and the conquistadors were lucky to receive Spanish reinforcements from that army, which had been disbanded in April 1526. For the next few years, Alvarado and his men were constantly under attack from the natives, but they managed to hold on before eventually quelling the rebellion by 1530. The Kaqchikel lords were executed for treason, and many of the settlements were destroyed.

After the deaths of thousands of natives, almost all of Guatemala was under Spanish rule by the 1530s. With northern Yucatán soon falling to Francisco de Montejo, the Maya civilization was being pressured from all sides. Indeed, the Spanish yoke seemed to be catastrophic for this once-thriving civilization. The *encomienda* system essentially enslaved tens of thousands of natives, who were unable to put up a fight against the colonizers. Many settlements were completely abandoned, as the population was forced to work in fields outside of the cities. The cultural transformation of the region was also evident from the very beginning. The natives were not forced to convert, but the gradual building of Christian churches and the domination of the colonizers took its toll on local religions and customs. Soon, most Mesoamericans had either converted to Catholicism or worshiped the Christian God alongside a plethora of their own gods in the pantheon.

The Yucatán and Guatemala were perhaps the hardest places to conquer, and the Maya people demonstrated an excellent capability to resist, even if they were eventually subjugated by the mid-16th century. The two conquistadors associated with the fall of the Maya in the region—Francisco de Montejo and Pedro de Alvarado—managed to crush the resistance they encountered and claimed the riches of the Yucatán and Guatemala for themselves. Still, there is much more to the conquest of what we today call Central America.

Conquest of Honduras

Above, we briefly mentioned several rival expeditions to claim the native lands in what is the modern-day country of Honduras. Last time we left off, Hernán Cortés, who was forced to travel there with a force to quell the rebellious conquistadors, was leaving almost empty-handed after a long and strenuous journey through the Maya Lowlands. In early 1526, when Cortés finally made contact with the Spanish in Honduras, he was informed that the threat of the rebelling Cristóbal de Olid, who had defied Cortés's orders, had been neutralized, prompting the latter to turn back to New Spain. However, the troubles in Honduras were far from over. Honduras was perhaps the most disputed area among the different conquistador groups, with each of them diverting their attention to establishing themselves as the rulers of this part of Central America.

The situation would escalate very soon after the departure of Cortés. Cortés fully believed that he had the right to rule Honduras, despite his unlucky expedition and the failure of the previous forces he had sent to take control of the region. By the time of his departure, most of what is modern-day Honduras was still up for grabs, and Cortés had the least credible claim to it. He did entrust the governance of the province to his cousin, Hernando de Saavedra, and the latter was more than happy to start exploring with his men, mostly focusing on the region of Olancho on the border of Nicaragua.

The problem with this was that the borders between the territories were not clearly defined. Saavedra and his men claimed the Olancho Valley but were almost immediately challenged by conquistadors from southern Mesoamerica, led by Pedro Arias Dávila (also known as Pedrarias Dávila). An experienced colonizer himself, he had mostly spent time exploring and conquering the Isthmus of Panama. He claimed the Olancho Valley for himself, knowing that controlling the territory meant more wealth and prestige in the region.

Dávila was a very cunning and zealous individual. He was a "classic" power-hungry conquistador who was ready to trample over anybody who stepped in his way. For more than a decade, he was the most important figure in southern Central America, controlling Panama and later consolidating his power in Nicaragua. There is not much to cover in these campaigns since they did not result in any extravagant ventures or overly significant material gains, like, for example, Cortés's expedition in Mexico.

When Pedro Arias Dávila moved more north, sending his men to the contested Olancho Valley, they bickered with Saavedra's men over the control of the area in 1526. A few skirmishes broke out, with neither side achieving anything significant. Eventually, both parties had to halt their efforts and stop the infighting for a serious reason: the Spanish Crown had decided to get more directly involved in colonial affairs. The Crown had heard of the disagreements between conquistadors and their supporters over disputed territories and chose its own representatives to arrive in the colonies with royal grants to govern and administer the lands. Thus, in October 1526, the new governor of Honduras, Diego López de Salcedo, arrived in the town of Trujillo to take control of the region and stop the infighting between the Spanish.

Salcedo sailed to Honduras from Santo Domingo with quite a lot of men and resources, and he was able to quickly take over power in the region from Saavedra. However, the new governor had an obvious flaw: he was unfamiliar with the matters of the New World. This was his first time in the Americas. He did not understand the relationship the Spanish had with the natives. In Spanish-controlled Honduras, just like in other colonies of the kingdom, the *encomienda* system was very prevalent, but it heavily relied upon the cooperation of the natives due to the numerical inferiority of the conquistadors. The colonizers simply did not have enough men to assert total dominance and control over the natives, but they were still allowed to impose their power due a multitude of reasons. For example, the natives knew of the disparity that existed militarily between themselves and the colonizers and had heard stories of what the Spanish were capable of doing to anyone who opposed them. There was also the divinity that some people attributed to the conquistadors, although this was rather rare in Mesoamerica. In any case, as long as the work the natives had to do in the *encomienda* was not much more labor-heavy and different than what they had done before the arrival of the colonizers, they were content to obey to avoid bloodshed and oppression.

Things changed in Honduras with the arrival of Salcedo, as the new governor was very strict in relation to the natives. He and his men actively discriminated against the local people, forcing them to work difficult jobs to maximize whatever profit there was to gain from the region. The situation got very bad very quickly. As soon as the new colonizers started to exploit the services and the will of the local population, the state of affairs escalated to a full-on rebellion in 1527, about half a year after Salcedo had landed in Trujillo. The rebels were ruthlessly dealt with, but that only incited more violence and disobedience. Salcedo proceeded to arrest the previous rulers of Honduras, sending them to Cuba to face the royal *audiencia*, but Saavedra and his crew managed to flee.

In addition to this, the new royal governor was confronted by the problem of Pedro Arias Dávila in Nicaragua, who had sent messengers to clear up the disputes that existed between the two camps. Instead of negotiating, as the borders were not clearly defined between the two colonies, Salcedo decided that it would be a good idea to forcefully claim the colony and assert his authority well beyond what had been intended for him. In short, the royal decision to appoint a new governor to Honduras seemed to be backfiring.

In the end, López de Salcedo would not be able to handle the pressure. On his way to Nicaragua with about 150 or so men, he managed to upset the natives even more, looting and burning their villages and forcing them to evacuate their dwellings. The pillaging of native settlements tired his men, and when the time came to confront Dávila's forces, the latter was able to easily defeat the governor of Honduras, taking him as prisoner. Not only that, but back in Trujillo, the conquistadors overthrew those he had left in command of the town.

Salcedo would be released after spending about a year as Dávila's prisoner, but it was only thanks to assistance from the Crown's other representatives and through rigorous mediation between him and Dávila, who officially became the governor of Nicaragua in July 1527. The terms of Salcedo's release involved setting new borders between Nicaragua and Honduras, and the royal decree that was drawn up finally resolved the dispute regarding the province of Olancho and other territories the two colonies shared. Upon Salcedo's release and return to Honduras in 1529, he was still hopeful of regaining control over the territory and wished to organize another expedition against the natives. However, he died due to an illness before he could proceed.

Just like that, the first royal appointee in Honduras proved to be a disappointment. From the year 1530 onward, the situation in the colony deteriorated even further, as Honduras almost fully slipped away from Spanish control. The conquistadors who remained in Trujillo, which was still the only town in the colony with only two hundred or so inhabitants, proceeded to elect their own governors instead of waiting for new royal representatives. This also proved to be a mistake. For the next few years, a complete state of chaos developed in Honduras, again due to the fact that many rival conquistadors struggled for power. In fact, no one really knew what was going on in the colony. In 1532, a new royal governor by the name of Diego Alvitez was assigned to the province. Alvitez met the same fate as all the other conquistadors in the position before him.

With different conquistador camps scattered around the country and the natives no longer under control, it was clear that to keep Honduras firmly under the grasp of Spain, an experienced leader was needed who had proven himself before. Pedro Arias Dávila had always floated around as a potential candidate to take over in Honduras due to his experience in Panama and Nicaragua. Dávila himself was adamant about expanding his role to include the governorship of Honduras. But he unexpectedly passed away in 1531, leaving the colonizers and the royal *audiencia* in need of another competent person.

None other than Pedro de Alvarado would become the new governor of Honduras, doing so in 1536. A veteran conquistador who had served with and remained loyal to Cortés, Alvarado had just managed to consolidate his position in Guatemala, defeating the Maya alliance against him. He was ready to move on to a new challenge. He did not have as many Spaniards in his force when he decided to march on Trujillo and establish himself as the new governor, but he did have a couple of thousand Maya warriors from the people he had conquered in the Guatemalan Highlands, which made things much easier. He was already well versed in conquering and then retaining control of the conquered, so he was able to easily emerge victorious over the natives in Honduras's Sula Valley. He was much more effective in quelling the resistance of the natives but preferred not to treat them as harshly as his predecessors, knowing that he needed their cooperation and loyalty in the future. Alvarado also achieved victories in Choloma, which is one of the largest cities in Honduras today, establishing *encomiendas* and forming amicable relations with the natives.

In nearly a year, Alvarado managed to consolidate Spanish control over the northern, central, and western parts of Honduras without having to compromise much. He was already the official governor of Guatemala, and he wished to add Honduras to his title. However, he was soon forced to travel to Spain when he learned that another distinguished and veteran conquistador, Francisco de Montejo, had obtained royal grants in 1534 for the colonization of Honduras.

Throughout all this time, Montejo had been busy unsuccessfully fighting in the Yucatán, as we have already covered, but he also challenged for the rights to Honduras. It took Montejo quite a lot of effort to finance his expedition to Honduras, which would arrive in late 1537. Upon his arrival, Montejo declared himself the new governor but was met with resistance from those loyal to Alvarado. The ambiguous situation forced Alvarado to travel to Spain to solve the dispute before the Crown, but the Crown decided in favor of Montejo to take over in 1540, although Alvarado was still granted the governorship of Guatemala for the next seven years.

By the year 1540, Alvarado had been absent from Honduras for three years, having consolidated the control of the colony with his men. During this time, Montejo was largely in charge in Honduras, despite not being liked by Alvarado's men. From the year 1540 onward, Montejo was affirmed by the royal court in Spain as the official governor of

Honduras, while Alvarado retained his governorship of Guatemala. The dispute over the control of Honduras was thus largely over, although it took the conquistadors many more years to fully claim the eastern part of the colony.

This whole situation of ambiguity, chaos, and anarchy, which had started in the 1520s, is a great example of the absence of rules and the existence of superficial boundaries in the early days of colonization. Different groups of conquistadors challenged each other for dominance in a completely unknown and remote setting to obtain glory and wealth. Colonization was essentially based on the principle of "first come, first serve," and while that was carried out more smoothly in some places, like Mexico, in most cases, the constant struggles between the Spanish set back their progress of conquering the New World.

The most tragic aspect of this was the fact that the natives suffered during all of this. Their dwellings were completely destroyed, and their friends and family members were massacred in combat, enslaved, or died due to previously unknown diseases that had been brought by the Spanish. The natives had to adapt to a completely new way of life under the colonizers. Natives only stood a realistic chance against the conquistadors when they could fully exploit their numerical superiority, but even then, it was unclear if they would flee once they heard the rumbling of cannons and guns and saw frenzied Spaniards mounted on horses.

Since the people living in Central America were less organized and did not have strong centralized states, it made it easier for the colonizers to exploit them. Had it not been for their own willingness to cooperate with each other, Central America would have fallen much quicker.

Chapter Five – Conquistadors in South America

First Contacts

Spanish colonial activities in South America were as just as extensive and influential in shaping the identity of the territory today as in North and Central America. The extent of Spanish possessions in South America would stretch from the northern and northeastern parts of the continent, around the Amazon rainforest and the modern-day territories of Brazil (colonized by Portugal), through the Pacific coast and the Andes Mountains to the southern part of Río de la Plata (mostly modern-day Argentina).

Portugal colonized eastern Brazil but refrained from going deeper into the continent and exploring the central and western parts due to the boundary that had been set by the papacy regarding colonial possessions in the New World. Although the Portuguese heavily exploited their colonies in South America, they focused their attention more on Africa and India, expanding there instead of challenging Spain and defying the papal bull. Thus, as was largely the matter with the conquests we have already discussed, Spain basically had a free hand in the colonization of South America, but getting the people of the continent under its control would prove to be far more difficult than expected.

The colonization of South America was an ongoing operation since the early days of colonization, running parallel to the campaigns in Mexico and Central America. In fact, the first person to spot the South

American lands was none other than Columbus himself, whose third expedition saw the mouth of the Orinoco River in the northeastern part of the continent. The main colonial activity in the early days of Spanish arrival would be concentrated in the northern and northwestern parts of South America, mainly in modern-day Panama and Colombia. An expedition led by Alonso de Ojeda first landed in modern-day Colombia at the Guajira Peninsula in mid-1502, but initial attempts to establish a Spanish settlement in the area failed due to the hostile nature of the natives. Columbus would make contact with the Chibcha people during his fourth voyage, during which he touched down in Honduras and then continued his journey south to Panama and northern Colombia.

After several more expeditions, which mostly explored the Isthmus of Panama and the point where it joined continental America, Vasco Núñez de Balboa and his men started to effectively colonize the area in 1509. Most Spanish settlements at this time were near the Caribbean coast, and different expeditions made landings at different points before continuing to explore. Balboa established himself in the town of Santa María de la Antigua Darien, located on the Caribbean coast in Colombia near the border of Panama.

After being elected as mayor of the town he had founded, Balboa soon distinguished himself thanks to his great administrative skills and ability to deal effectively with problems the Spanish inhabitants faced. From Santa María, he moved north along the coast, defeating the natives who resisted him or befriending and converting them to Christianity. By the year 1513, he had reached the town of Careta in modern-day Panama before briefly heading back to Santa María to replenish his men.

In the autumn of 1513, he set out on another expedition in the same direction but turned west from Careta, crossing the Isthmus before finally reaching the Pacific Ocean. This new unexplored sea excited Balboa and his men, and the conquistador called his discovery the South Sea, claiming it in the name of the Spanish Crown. Of course, he was unaware that what he discovered was, in fact, the largest body of water on Earth. During his expedition, Balboa encountered different Chibcha tribes and was forced to fight them on many occasions. Still, with the valuables he had taken from the natives, as well as pearls from the South Sea, he returned to Santa María, where he was hailed as a true explorer.

Santa María and other Spanish settlements founded on the Caribbean coast, near the Colombia-Panama border and around the Gulf of Urabá, were organized in 1513 into a new administrative division by the name of Castilla del Oro by King Ferdinand of Spain. Because of Balboa's expeditions, new territories in Panama were added to Castilla del Oro, and upon his return to Santa María, it seemed that he would continue to be the main figure in the region. However, when he returned back to northern Colombia in 1514, he was confronted by a new royally appointed governor, Pedro Arias Dávila, a figure we briefly talked about above. Pedro Arias Dávila had arrived with a large crew of over 1,500 conquistadors and 17 ships from Spain and was ready to take over the governorship and leadership of Castilla del Oro from Balboa.

The latter could do little to resist and was forced to give up his title and leave Santa María in search of his own glory to the north, organizing a small-scale expedition to Panama to explore the lands that lay north of the town of Careta. In 1519, Dávila summoned Balboa, tricking the conquistador to come to him and charging him with treason. Balboa denied the charges but was nevertheless arrested and executed alongside his sympathizers. This development earned Pedro Arias Dávila his infamy. He took over control of Castilla del Oro and organized several more expeditions to the north and the south, going deep into the western part of South America before getting involved in the struggles for Honduras, as we have already seen.

Pushing into Colombia

The colonization of South America continued, with modern-day Colombia becoming the main focus of the conquistadors, who founded numerous cities like Cartagena, Malambo, and Sincelejo in the decades following the initial exploration of the Caribbean coast. For the first fifteen years or so after the imprisonment and execution of Balboa, the conquistadors' main strategy was consolidating their holdings on the coast by setting up permanent settlements and surrounding them with *encomienda*. The Chibcha people who occupied the territories taken over by Castilla del Oro submitted to the colonizers. They had not formed a united political entity to be able to better defend themselves from the foreigners, and they did not possess the military capabilities to resist the might of Spanish gunpowder.

Still, despite taking over the northern South American lands, the conquistadors were not content with what they had gained. They had heard stories of kingdoms in the mountains bordering these lands that were full of gold and were far more powerful than the tribes they had easily subjugated. So, it was natural that many different expeditions were launched to find out the location of these promised lands.

As the conquistadors went deeper into Colombia, they encountered the people of the Muisca Confederation, located in the area of the Andean highlands known as Altiplano Cundiboyacense. The Muisca were far more complex than the Chibcha. Firstly, they had a more advanced political structure. The Muisca Confederation was an alliance between several tribes of the area, each headed by their own *cacique* (leader), who occupied different positions and governed different areas of life. For example, the *psihipqua* (*zipa*) was the most powerful. He was the equivalent of a king and was believed to possess divine abilities. He was respected and feared in the Muisca, almost to the point of idolization. The *iraca*, on the other hand, was the religious leader of the Muisca, who were based in what is now the city of Sogamoso, a sacred center where the most important ceremonies and rituals were held. Sogamoso housed the Temple of the Sun, the dwelling of the *iraca* and one of the most important places to the Muisca. Other *caciques* were in charge of different territories, but none of them had the power or authority to fully influence others. The Muisca were in a sort of defensive alliance with each other, something that came to be handy when the Spanish arrived.

The Muisca Confederation.
Milenioscuro, CC BY-SA 3.0 <https://creativecommons.org/licenses/by-sa/3.0>, via Wikimedia Commons; https://commons.wikimedia.org/wiki/File:Mapa_del_Territorio_Muisca.svg

What is even more exciting about the Muisca is their culture and societal structure. The most striking thing here is the fact that the Muisca society does not appear to have been traditionally hereditary, as was the case almost everywhere else in the New World. Instead, leadership passed to the leader's eldest nephew, the son of his sister, something that seems odd at first glance but signifies the complex family relationships between the Muisca. They worshiped a diverse pantheon of gods, and their religion and rituals were very interesting, as they were far more complex than those of their neighbors in the north. For example, one of the rituals probably included the *zipa* covering himself in gold, lying in a boat, and floating alone on Lake Guatavita to offer the gold to the gods. Meanwhile, his servants threw valuables into the lake. According to some historians, the famous legend of El Dorado—a mythical kingdom of gold—comes from the Spanish encountering this ritual.

In addition to the compelling polytheism and excessive ritualistic lifestyle of the Muisca, their culture was also advanced in other ways. Pottery, textile production, and agriculture were some of the most important activities of their society, with these activities being undertaken by both men and women. Astrology was another distinctive field where the natives excelled; they had designed their own calendars and were able to accurately pinpoint stars, to the excitement of the colonizers. Warfare was also a large part of their social life. The Muisca were surrounded by hostile tribes on all sides, especially the Muzo people from the east, who were famous for mining emeralds. Muisca men were assigned to the warrior class and were responsible for waging defensive wars against those who challenged them. The Muisca warriors covered themselves with symbols depicting their ancestors during fighting. They were fearsome in battle and utilized complex strategies and tactics.

When the Spanish established a permanent foothold in the northern part of modern-day Colombia, they started planning their expeditions to the south, avoiding the Amazon rainforest and diverting their attention to the mountainous regions of western South America. The expedition that would encounter the Muisca was led by Gonzalo Jiménez de Quesada, alongside his brother Hernán Pérez, and would embark from the town of Santa Marta in 1536. Of course, other expeditions in the Americas were already underway by this time, with one of the most notable led by Francisco Pizarro (something we will cover extensively later on). The reason behind the departure of Quesada and his expedition was probably the legends of El Dorado, but this seemingly exciting justification of discovering a promised land full of gold was nothing new. The conquistadors were always in search of gold. The legendary accounts of El Dorado simply served as an additional stimulus to the Spaniards, filling their journey with more purpose.

The Quesada brothers and their men set out from Santa Marta in April 1536 with about eight hundred conquistadors. They marched south and eventually reached the Colombian Andes Mountains. A common and logical strategy was to follow the river, the Magdalena, upstream since the tribes usually lived in the vicinity of a river. However, once the expedition entered the highlands, it started to encounter more and more problems. The terrain was too difficult to cross with horses, especially when the conquistadors got to the modern-day province of Tamalameque, where tens of small lakes are situated as an extension of the riverbed. Lives were lost trying to navigate these waters, and those who survived only managed to continue the journey about a month later after regrouping. Crucially, the two natives whom Quesada had brought along to serve as interpreters and guides also died, and the expedition was forced to continue without them in unknown territories.

After going farther to the south, the conquistadors reached the settlement of Chiriguaná, where they were able to quickly assert their dominance over the indigenous people and decided to stay to replenish their supplies. However, their stay at Chiriguaná was plagued by constant attacks from other natives, who sailed up the river with their canoes and fired deadly poisonous arrows, causing the expedition to lose more men. In addition, the dense forests of the area also housed other threats like deadly mosquitoes and spiders, and the conquistadors had to always keep an eye out for them.

By late 1536, the conquistadors were able to reach as far south as the modern-day city of Barrancabermeja, a small settlement that the conquistadors took with ease. Spirits were much lower at Barrancabermeja than they were at the beginning of the expedition. Gonzalo Jiménez de Quesada thus decided to break up his men, sending those who were wounded or weakened home and continuing on with the healthy men. About a hundred or so Spaniards were sent back. The expedition was reduced by almost half its original number. But the men reluctantly continued the march south.

Deciding to abandon the tropical lowlands, Quesada took his men a bit to the east, entering the highlands, where they would encounter signs of indigenous life. In February 1537, just when many of the conquistadors were inclined to abandon the expedition, Quesada's vanguard reached the Muisca settlement of Chipatá, located high up in the Colombian Andes. The Muisca greeted the colonizers and allowed them to stay for a couple of months, voluntarily giving them provisions. Chipatá's inhabitants even let the Spanish priest hold a Christian sermon in their village, which they curiously observed and took part in. Instead of looting the small village and imposing themselves on the natives, the conquistadors cooperated with the friendly Muisca and stayed with them for quite a while. Quesada and his men learned more about the tribe and the larger confederation, whose center lay farther to the southeast. Motivated by the natives' stories about rich rulers and great temples full of gold, the conquistadors believed they had gotten a lead on El Dorado and started preparing to set out in hopes of getting to their destination.

The Conquest of the Muisca

In March 1537, the conquistadors reached the heartland of the Muisca Confederation and were very excited to see the level of development in the natives. The architectural style of the tribal settlements, the vast farm fields, the arts, and the ceramic work they encountered in the Muisca towns were amazing. But since there were no signs of golden buildings, the Spanish settlers pressed forward, closing in on the southern Muisca capital of Bacatá. They journeyed south and traversed the Ubaté-Chiquinquirá Valley. Guided by the winding Suárez River, they pressed on, eventually reaching the serene shores of Lake Fúquene. As the Spanish soldiers drew closer to Bacatá, they found the *caciques* of the settlements Simijaca, Fúquene, and Tausa to be fiercely loyal to the *zipa*. Fueled by a thirst for riches, the conquistadors pressed on. Along the way, they founded a couple of towns and imposed their rule on the natives when they resisted.

The expedition continued to the important salt-producing town of Nemocón, where they were greeted with gifts of food, including new delicacies like deer, pigeons, and guinea pigs. However, their peace was short-lived, as they faced their first attack from the Muisca warriors. Undeterred, the Spanish soldiers emerged victorious and set their sights on the Bogotá savanna, where they encountered the fertile plains dotted with more farm fields. Quesada was enamored with the pleasant climate, and he named the flatlands the Valle de los Alcázares.

Then, he led his reduced army of 170 men toward Funza, the domain of the *zipa*. Despite facing hundreds of Muisca warriors, the superior arms of the Spanish soldiers proved unbeatable. The *caciques* believed the invaders were divine and hesitated to attack. Funza was conquered and founded as a Spanish town on April 20th, 1537, marking the end of a grueling journey that claimed the lives of a couple of hundred soldiers. Of the original crew that set out from Santa Marta a year prior, only 162 survivors remained.

Supposedly, Tisquesusa, one of the Muisca rulers, had a revelation about the ominous arrival of the Spanish conquerors. He had been visited in his dream and was told of foreign invaders who would cause his bloody demise. When Tisquesusa was alerted to the Spanish army's advance, he dispatched a cunning spy to Suesca to gather intel on the enemy's weaponry, strength, and potential for defeat. In response to the looming threat, Tisquesusa abandoned the capital Bacatá and sought refuge in the fortifications of Nemocón.

This strategic move lured the Spanish troops directly into a trap, where they were ambushed by a fierce army of over six hundred Muisca warriors. But the *zipa* soon realized that his warriors stood no chance against the advanced weapons of the Spanish. With a heavy heart, Tisquesusa returned to Bacatá and ordered the evacuation of the capital, leaving it a ghost town for the conquistadors to discover. Undeterred, the Spanish set out to find Tisquesusa, launching a daring night attack in the vicinity of Facatativá.

The conquistadors continued their advance in the Muisca territories, crossing over to the northern part and splitting up their forces to scout out different settlements and maximize their gains. Although they managed to accumulate a lot of loot throughout the journey and found gold in the Muisca settlements, it was slowly becoming apparent that the legend of El Dorado might have been a product of exaggeration. Still, the conquistadors believed they had merely missed the golden city this time, thinking they had diverted from their original path. Despite this, they were more than happy to pillage and loot the Muisca towns, especially those located in the northwest, which contained emeralds and other valuable stones.

With the *zipa* of Bacatá defeated, many of the southern Muisca complied with Spanish demands and supplied the foreigners with provisions, extending their stay in the land. The imposition of Spanish rule in these areas was, at first, superficial since no good links existed between it and the rest of the colonial settlements in northern South America. As the conquistadors pressed on, they slowly entered the northern part of the confederation, which was ruled by the *zaque* or *hoa* in the native town of Hunza (Tunja). Upon their arrival, the conquistadors were confronted with messengers sent by Quemuenchatocha, the *zaque* who was not keen on the invaders. He tasked his men to try and make peace with the conquistadors and find out what they were after in these lands, as this was the first encounter the northern Muisca had with the Europeans. Quesada and his men informed the chief they had been searching for a golden palace, prompting the latter to try and hide his riches before hostilities could break out between the natives and the foreigners.

Quemuenchatocha believed he could defend Hunza and his surroundings, but he was defeated relatively easily in August 1537 and was captured alongside some of the more important members of his retinue. The conquistadors noticed the lavish attire of their prisoners and tortured them for days in the hopes that they would give up the location of their valuables. Quemuenchatocha was eventually released, but the power in the northern Muisca Confederation would be assumed by his nephew, Aquiminzaque, who would emerge as the last *zaque* of the Muisca.

The young ruler tried to cooperate with the Spanish to avoid further war and bloodshed, even converting to Christianity and sending lavish gifts to please the conquistadors. Still, he ultimately ruled as a puppet of Quesada and his men. When he tried to organize some form of resistance, he was imprisoned and publicly executed in 1540. The rest of the important rulers of neighboring towns and tribes were also executed. By then, Hunza was firmly under Spanish control, as reinforcements arrived from the northern colonies to bolster conquistador forces in the area and expand the *encomienda* system.

Before the execution of Aquiminzaque and the consolidation of Spanish control over the Muisca Confederation, Gonzalo Jiménez Quesada's expedition continued to the holy site of Sogamoso, which was home to the last *iraca* by the name of Sugamuxi. The conquistadors arrived at the town in late August or early September and proceeded straight to the Temple of the Sun, the main religious building in the Muisca territories. They looted the temple, taking a couple of hundred kilograms worth of golden artifacts, as well as countless other valuables, before setting the temple on fire and reducing it to ashes. One Spanish account actually calls the burning of the Temple of the Sun an accident caused by the recklessness of some conquistadors who got too close to the wooden building with lit torches. In any case, the most impressive structure of the Muisca was destroyed by the conquistadors in the autumn of 1537, but the loot taken from it still did not quite meet the expectations of the famed El Dorado.

By 1538, most of the powerful *caciques* of the Muisca Confederation had been defeated by Quesada's expedition, with the conquistadors having accumulated a considerable number of riches through their activities. They divided the wealth among themselves and returned back to the center of the confederation to consolidate their control, having learned that other expeditions were also closing in on the Muisca territories. In mid-1538, they founded the city of Bogotá (the capital of modern-day Colombia), which they dubbed after the town of Bacatá, the residence of the southern *zipa*. Soon, they would organize the former Muisca territories and incorporate them with other northern colonies, forming the New Kingdom of Granada (after the birthplace of the Quesada brothers in Granada, Andalusia), which eventually became a viceroyalty of Spain.

The account of the conquest of the Muisca survives mainly through a book written in the 1550s, *Epitome de la conquista del Nuevo Reino de Granada*. Although the author is not known, the book is attributed to Gonzalo Jiménez de Quesada.

After the conquest of the Muisca, Quesada would meet up with the leaders of other expeditions in modern-day Colombia, Sebastián de Belalcázar and Nikolaus de Federmann. They agreed on the administrative matters of the newly conquered territories and decided to sail back to Spain to obtain royal approval and privileges. The three would leave the New World in 1539. Having set up Bogotá as the center of operations in New Granada, the objective of the conquistadors and the Spanish Crown was to consolidate their position in the region and properly colonize the natives, assimilating them into European culture and society.

Since the early 1540s, more and more Spaniards settled in Colombia, greatly increasing its population and contributing to the establishment of more *encomiendas*, which transformed the life of the native population just as much as it had in other parts of the Americas. The indigenous people slowly converted to Catholicism, and signs of the old Muisca religion and culture soon faded, as the Crown placed more emphasis on the evangelization of the conquered "heathens" and their enlightenment of the principles of Christ. The Spanish also brought European crops with them. These crops were previously unknown to the indigenous people of South America, and they were able to successfully grow them in the fertile lands of the Altiplano. A large mining industry was also organized in the mountainous regions of the old Muisca territories, with the Spanish extracting valuable minerals and metals from the Colombian Andes and growing the economy of the colony.

In short, the conquest of the Muisca Confederation, although often overlooked when compared to other endeavors of the conquistadors, was a vital part of the Spanish conquest of the Americas. The Muisca civilization was one of the first more advanced civilizations the Spaniards encountered in South America. The takeover of the former Muisca lands and the slow domination of the indigenous people provided the conquistadors with an immense influx of riches and one of the most important colonial holdings in the New World, New Granada, which, over time, became a stable part of the growing Spanish Empire.

Chapter Six – The Spanish Conquest of the Inca

The Inca Empire

We now turn our attention to the story of another one of the most (in)famous conquests by the Spanish in the New World: the conquest of the Inca Empire by Francisco Pizarro. The conquest of the Inca is fascinating for several reasons. The scale of the Spanish expedition that resulted in the subjugation of the Inca and the destruction of the Inca Empire, located mostly in modern-day Peru, is comparable with that of Cortés's expedition into the lands of the Aztecs.

Just like the Aztecs of Mexico, the Inca of Peru were a very complex civilization with their own distinct sociocultural makeup that distinguished them from other people in the New World. At its height, the Inca Empire stretched along the Andes Mountains from modern-day western Colombia south to central Chile and western Argentina, making it the most consolidated state of indigenous peoples in South America. The Inca are often regarded as the most interesting of the Andean civilizations. The conquest of the Inca greatly increased the power of Spain and significantly elevated its position in the New World.

Before we recount the story of how Francisco Pizarro and other conquistadors managed to defeat the natives and emerge as the masters of the Andes, it is worth looking at the overall makeup of the Inca Empire and a brief history of its rise to power.

Like the Aztec Empire, the Inca Empire was relatively new in the 16th century when the European colonizers first encountered it, although the region of the Andes Mountains, where the Inca were based, had been inhabited by different people groups for thousands of years. In the pre-Colombian era (that is, before the arrival of Columbus in the New World in the late 15th century), two empires preceded the emergence of the Inca Empire in the Andes: the Tiwanaku in the south, centered around Lake Titicaca and the main city of Tiwanaku, and the Wari (Huari) in the north, located chiefly in modern-day Peru. Both of these political entities are thought to have slowly grown beginning around 100 CE. They eventually fell in the 10th century, more than four hundred years before the Spanish conquest of the region. The Tiwanaku and the Wari are often considered the pioneers of a more complex form of civilization in the Andes. They were responsible for implementing many of the practices the neighboring peoples and eventually the Inca would inherit, like exceptional forms of agriculture and road-building.

As for the Inca themselves, they were a relatively small tribe by the beginning of the 12th century, inhabiting central Peru. Legend tells of a man by the name of Manco Cápac (Manqu Qhapaq), also known as Manco Inca, which roughly translates from the local Quechua language to "the first emperor" or "the first royal." According to Inca mythology, Manco Cápac is responsible for the foundation of the city of Cusco (Cuzco) and is the first ruler of the Inca. In the legend, he is given a divine origin, being the son of the sun god Inti, who gave him a golden javelin, and the moon goddess Mama Quilla.

Manco Cápac emerged from the cave of Paqariq Tampu and threw his golden javelin in the air. He founded the city of Cusco where it landed and constructed the Temple of the Sun in the name of Inti, which was located in the south-central part of modern-day Peru. According to another narrative, Manco Cápac was a tribal leader who conquered the people of the Cusco Valley with the help of his brothers. The golden javelin appears in this version as well, but it was given to him by his father (who was not the chief deity). After defeating the neighboring tribes and establishing himself at Cusco, Manco Cápac then imprisoned and killed his brothers, married his sister Mama Ocllo, and emerged as the first Sapa Inca (king) of the Kingdom of Cusco, which would eventually become the Inca Empire.

Whatever the case, the Kingdom of Cusco appears to have been established by the 13th century, but it started to grow dramatically in size in the early 15th century under Pachacuti Inca Yupanqui. His son, Túpac, continued the conquest and consolidation of neighboring tribes, essentially growing the empire to the borders it held by the time of the Spanish arrival.

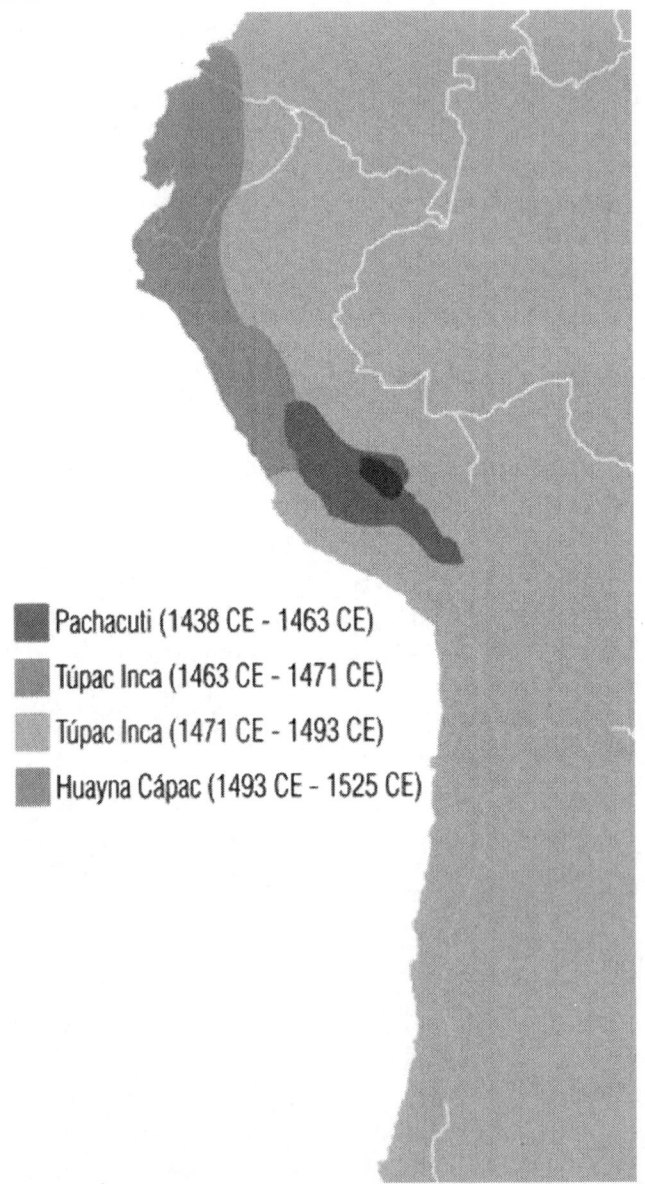

A look at how the Inca Empire expanded over time.
QQuantum, CC BY-SA 4.0 <https://creativecommons.org/licenses/by-sa/4.0>, via Wikimedia Commons; https://commons.wikimedia.org/wiki/File:Inca_Expansion.svg

The Sapa Inca was the supreme ruler of the empire, although the title was not considered to have been necessarily hereditary in the beginning. The eldest son of the Sapa Inca would usually have to go through a set of difficult challenges and training, both physical and mental, which were said to have been designed by the gods. Only after passing these tests would he be named the next ruler. As the absolute ruler, the Sapa Inca had virtually no limits to his power and was involved in all aspects of life in the empire. Due to his importance, he was considered to possess divine attributes; after all, they were seen as descendants of the god Inti. The role of the Sapa Inca was expressed by the lavish attire he wore—a special mantle and headband decorated with the royal insignia—and the special accessories he carried, like a golden scepter or a spear with feathers.

During the rule of Pachacuti Inca, at the beginning of Inca expansion, the city of Cusco assumed a far more important role as the main political and religious center of the growing empire. However, as the Inca expanded, a complex political system was implemented that still amazes historians to this day due to its complicated, highly bureaucratized nature, which was unlike the other civilizations of the region. The Inca lands were divided into four administrative entities called *suyus*: Antisuyu in the east, Collasuyu in the south, Cuntinsuyu in the west, and Chinchanysuyu in the north, all four surrounding the capital of Cusco. Each *suyu* was then divided into smaller *wamani*, the Inca equivalent of European provinces.

Such a thorough administrative division of the empire was a clever way of effectively managing millions of subjects under the rule of the Sapa Inca. The heads of the *wamani* were responsible for collecting the taxes of their respective areas, giving the money to the governors of the four *suyus,* the *apu,* who accumulated the wealth and provided it to the capital, which was directly governed by the Sapa Inca. Essentially, the Inca were organized as a federalist state. If we make the comparison to the modern-day US, the *suyus* were basically states, while Cusco was its own entity, much like Washington, DC. The system was effective, as it was able to maintain cohesiveness and stability.

The complex political structure was also supported by an equally complicated administrative office system. The Sapa Inca, as we have already mentioned, was the supreme head of the state, having a say in all major affairs of the empire and also enjoying his position as a divine being since he was a descendant of the gods. The second person of importance in Inca society was the high priest, the highest-standing religious figure. Following him was the Inca Rantin, who essentially acted as the hand of the king or the grand vizier. After that, different administrative offices were filled by people of noble birth.

Besides the political and administrative makeup of the Inca, what catches the eye about this Andean civilization is just the sheer level of development in all other aspects of life compared to its South American and Mesoamerican neighbors. This is made even more impressive when considering the difficult, mountainous terrain of the Andes, where the civilization flourished. The Inca cities, the largest of which were home to tens of thousands of inhabitants, were mostly located on hilltops a couple of thousand meters high and were almost fully built in stone. This is remarkable because it was very difficult to undertake projects of such magnitude and complexity with the tools of the age and also because living permanently in such high altitudes is not suited for most people. Modern studies have shown the Inca descendants and the people who live in the Andean Highlands adapted to the height of their homes biologically, having developed a larger lung capacity and double the amount of oxygen-transporting hemoglobin. The most amazing cities of the Inca, besides the capital of Cusco, were Huánuco Pampa and Machu Picchu. Their ruins survive today, attracting countless tourists and reminding them of the ingenuity of Inca architecture and engineering.

The cities of the Inca were interconnected by an amazing paved road system, running about twenty-five thousand miles in total, which allowed for easier access between them and for the establishment of trade routes. Their trade was very developed, as different regions of the empire specialized in the production of different goods. However, money was not used in the exchanges. Instead, a barter system was implemented.

Ceramics, pottery, and textile manufacturing were all popular industries in the Inca Empire, but agriculture played a central role. Thanks to their advanced system of elevated agricultural fields, which were organized in terraces, and the irrigation channels that ran through them to provide enough water in places with low precipitation, agriculture flourished, emerging as a cornerstone of the Inca civilization's economy. Farming tools were developed enough to allow for the production of a large number of crops, even in difficult terrain, again emphasizing the adaptive nature of the Inca to their environment and climate.

The infrastructure also provided the Inca rulers with the ability to better govern their subjects and to allow for the quick and effective exchange of information. Traveling was mostly done by foot or on llamas, which were domesticated and widely used in Inca society. (Surprisingly, for being people of such complexity and development, the Inca never quite implemented the usage of the wheel in their lives, probably due to the mountainous nature of the environment they lived in.) Thousands of rope bridges were also constructed to make sure that the sides of canyons and ditches were also connected.

All in all, many historians regard the Inca civilization to have been the most organized and advanced, not only in South America but arguably in all of the New World as well. Their level of development when it came to administrative affairs is even said to have rivaled some early medieval European nations. With an effective federalist system that still allowed for the centralization of power to lay in the hands of the Sapa Inca, the empire maintained stability while steadily growing throughout the 15th century, reaching its peak just before the discovery of the Americas by Christopher Columbus. On paper, the Inca were the most suited to successfully resist the imposition of European power, owing not only to their advanced sociopolitical state but also to the easily defendable geography of the area they inhabited. However, the arrival of the conquistador expeditions into the Inca realm coincided with an unlucky period of internal crisis within the empire. A civil war between the contenders to the throne ultimately weakened the cohesiveness of the Inca, giving an additional advantage to the foreigners.

Francisco Pizarro

Portrait of Francisco Pizarro *by Amable-Paul Coutan.*
https://en.wikipedia.org/wiki/File:Portrait_of_Francisco_Pizarro.jpg

Francisco Pizarro is perhaps just as well known as Hernán Cortés, and for good reason. Nowadays, Pizarro often gets attributed with the crowning achievement of having defeated the Inca, taking the riches of Peru and the Andes for Spain. Although this assertion is mostly true, when looking at the larger picture, many questions arise, especially when it comes to his comparison with Hernán Cortés. The most obvious difference between the two is the fact that Cortés was the man responsible for fully destroying the Aztec Empire and establishing a strong foothold for Spain in modern-day central and southern Mexico. Historians agree that the Aztec Empire collapsed with the conquest of Tenochtitlan in 1521. Pizarro, on the other hand, did lead the conquistadors and was a chief actor during the struggles against the Inca, but he only managed to conquer the South American empire to a certain extent. His efforts led to the initial takeover of the Inca by the conquistadors, but as we will come to see, internal strife between the Spanish, stern resistance from the Inca, and Pizarro's murder in 1541 made the conquest of the Inca Empire far more complicated and drawn-out.

Although the territory formerly controlled by the Inca was seized by the Spanish by the 1540s, it would be about thirty years later, in 1572, that the last Inca heir, Túpac Amaru, would meet his end at the hands of the Spanish, putting an end to the "conquest" of the Inca.

Before we move on to how Pizarro and others managed to establish Spanish control in this part of South America, we should first take a look at the former's career as a conquistador, something that often eludes public discussion since it is overshadowed by his later triumphs.

Pizarro began his conquistador activities in 1509, having joined Alonso de Ojeda, a man we briefly mentioned above, in the latter's third exploratory endeavor. In November 1509, Ojeda and his men entered the Gulf of Urabá in northern Colombia but failed to establish a self-sustaining colony and soon departed. After temporarily returning to Spain and trying his luck in colonial affairs again, Pizarro eventually ended up in the crew of Vasco Núñez de Balboa, accompanying him in the expedition that crossed Panama to reach the Pacific Ocean in 1513.

However, as the power dynamics in Castilla del Oro became more complicated with the arrival of Pedro Arias Dávila, Pizarro chose to ally with the latter, realizing that he would emerge on top in the struggle against Balboa. In fact, Pizarro was among the men who arrested Balboa, and for his loyalty and support, he was awarded the mayorship of the city of Panama for a while in 1519.

During his tenure as the mayor of Panama, Pizarro became interested in a potential expedition down the western coast of South America. This was because of a semi-successful campaign that had been undertaken by some conquistadors in 1522, who reached the coast of Peru and sailed back to the Spanish colonies after encountering natives who were in possession of gold and valuable minerals. The stories of the distant land of Piru, as it was originally referred to, became very popular in the Spanish colony of Castilla del Oro. The stories also caught Pizarro's attention. The narrative coincided with the later notions of El Dorado, a city of gold located somewhere in the western part of South America, a region that was still unexplored by the conquistadors in the 1520s.

At the same time, the news of the conquest of Tenochtitlan and the fall of the Aztec Empire spread throughout the Spanish colonies, motivating many to try their luck in exploration, knowing that it brought fame and wealth. So, after some consideration, the expedition-hungry Pizarro, who had been disappointed with his previous travels due to the modesty of loot, decided he wanted to embark on a journey down the Pacific coast of South America. He found like-minded individuals who were motivated by the search for golden cities and unafraid of what the journey might have in store for them. Diego de Almagro and a priest by the name of Hernando de Luque were some of the few who joined up. Pizarro petitioned Governor Pedro Arias, asking him for the resources necessary for the expedition.

In November 1524, Pizarro embarked on his first expedition to Peru, sailing south with about eighty men. However, this journey proved unsuccessful, as the conquistadors were stopped short of their desired goal due to severely bad weather and the lack of provisions. Once the conquistadors tried to disembark on the western coast of the continent, they were confronted by hostile natives, sparking a skirmish that forced them to go back. The natives Pizarro and his men encountered were probably the Quitu people, who were already under the jurisdiction and control of the Inca Empire.

The expedition sailed back to Panama empty-handed, but the men's fervor had not yet faded. In 1526, they managed to obtain permission from the new governor in charge of Panama, Pedro de los Ríos, as Pedro Arias Dávila was busy with his endeavors in Nicaragua and other parts of Central America. Pizarro embarked on his second journey to Peru in the same year, this time having well over one hundred men.

The expedition reached the mouth of the San Juan River in modern-day Colombia, where a part of the crew decided to stay with Pizarro to explore the shores while Almagro sailed back to Panama to get reinforcements and supplies. A contingent of the conquistadors who stayed with Pizarro ventured south, eventually coming across a group of natives who carried emeralds, some gold, and textiles. Believing they had found proof of the riches of the region, the Spaniards captured the natives and took them back to their captain.

Pizarro and his men struggled to survive in the unknown and inhospitable lands of tropical Colombia. Almagro returned with reinforcements, something that came as a relief to Pizarro. It was then decided that Almagro should be sent back again to get more men and supplies, and he was given the valuables the expedition had found as proof of the expedition's success and potential.

Meanwhile, Pizarro and his men relocated farther south, trying to make headway but again struggling to continue the expedition and sustaining many losses. The natives they encountered in these areas, probably somewhere in modern-day northern Ecuador, were very hostile. And back in Panama, Almagro failed to gather more men for the expedition, as the new governor had been reluctant to send more funds to something that had yielded so little.

Instead of allowing Almagro to sail back with more men and provisions, he sent his own two ships, charging them with bringing back Pizarro and the conquistadors to avoid the loss of more lives. In early 1527, the governor's men reached Pizarro, but the latter was not ready to let his men just sail back after all the progress they had made (at least, he saw them as making progress). Many of his crewmates thought otherwise and decided to leave for Panama. Only thirteen men remained with Pizarro. They were left behind for seven months, relocating to the island of Gorgona off the coast of Colombia. Throughout this period, Pizarro and his "famous thirteen" somehow survived, devoid of all contact with the natives and other conquistadors. Blinded by their ultimate goal, they still were not ready to give up.

Fortune was on Pizarro's side this time, as Almagro somehow managed to get a hold of another ship and a small crew to sail to the island and rescue the conquistadors in the spring of 1528. The sight of

Almagro heightened the spirits of the conquistadors, who decided to go for a final push south before returning to Panama. In April, they boarded the ship and sailed down the coast, eventually ending up in the region of Tumbes in northwestern Peru, where they disembarked to scout the territory. The conquistadors roughly mapped the coast to the best of their ability, naming several places to act as a reference for their eventual return. They spotted the coastal settlements of the natives but decided not to approach them as a group since it might cause a poor reaction from the inhabitants.

After making sure that the people they had seen were, in fact, in the possession of gold, and after being amazed by the domesticated llamas, Pizarro and his men decided to turn back to Panama in the hopes that they would someday return and claim the riches that awaited them. Before they left Tumbes in the late spring of 1528, they took a native boy with them, who would be baptized and named Felipillo. He spoke the local Quechua language and quickly learned basic Spanish. Felipillo acted as an interpreter and guide in Pizarro's later journeys, assuming a similar role in Pizarro's expeditions as La Malinche had with Cortés.

The conquistadors returned to Panama in 1528, but Pizarro was again denied permission for another expedition to Peru. Instead of trying to obtain the rights by arguing with the governor, Pizarro and his associates devised a plan to appeal to a much higher authority: the Spanish Crown. It seemed like a logical decision, and Pizarro sailed to Spain in 1529, requesting a royal audience with King Charles V. He took whatever gold and silver he had gotten in Peru as proof and was probably accompanied by Felipillo to further reinforce his case.

He arrived in Europe in the summer, but it would actually be Queen Isabella who granted Pizarro the right to colonize Peru since the king was unavailable. The royal document granted the conquistador a great deal of authority, naming him the *adelantado*, the governor and captain general of the territories he explored on the western coast of South America.

Excited, Pizarro set out to assemble men who wished to accompany him on the adventure, raising about 180 men in Spain. He left Europe in early 1530. After arriving in Panama, Pizarro soon left for his third and final expedition to Peru in December 1530, forever changing the course of history.

The Inca Civil War

In the 1520s, Pizarro and the other conquistadors made contact with the peripheral regions of the Inca Empire, although they did not know that the tribes they saw in modern-day Ecuador were part of a far more organized and complex political entity whose center was more to the south. However, before Pizarro's third expedition to the Inca lands, the conquistadors accidentally caused something that created problems for the Inca. During their visit to Tumbes, where the Spaniards came in close contact with the natives, they passed along a deadly European novelty: smallpox, a destructive disease that decimated the populations in Mexico and Mesoamerica. Smallpox eventually spread in the northern part of the Inca Empire, and its effects were just as horrible.

Smallpox likely caused the death of Sapa Inca Huayna Cápac, who is thought to have contracted the disease during his visit to Ecuador. Huayna Cápac never had any contact with the Spanish, but he became very ill in the mid-1520s, just around the time the conquistadors arrived in the lands of the Inca. So, it is not unlikely that he was just one of the millions of victims who fell prey to the diseases the Europeans brought to the Americas.

Whatever the cause of Huayna Cápac's death might have been, it led to a series of events that significantly weakened the Inca Empire and indirectly helped the conquistadors to conquer it in the 1530s. The Sapa Inca was a powerful ruler, and it had been thanks to him that the empire had become so prosperous and powerful, having expanded the Inca realm to its largest borders. He mainly focused on the expansion of the Inca Empire to the north, absorbing the people of what is modern-day Ecuador into the confederation and marrying the queen of Quito. But upon his death, a succession struggle sparked between his sons, leading to the Inca Civil War, which lasted from 1529 to 1532.

When Huayna Cápac died, his eldest son, Huáscar, was supported by most of the important forces inside the empire. Huáscar's mother was the sister and wife of Huayna Cápac, making him of purer blood. The Inca placed a lot of emphasis on retaining the purity of blood, and incestuous relationships within the royal family were common. Huáscar also had ruled in the central-southern part of the empire near Cusco during his father's lifetime of his father and was thus recognized by the Inca nobility, despite the fact that he reportedly was very cunning and unlawful. Still, his legitimacy earned him the throne, which he claimed with the support of his loyal followers in 1529.

On the other hand, there was Atahualpa, the second of Huayna's sons. He was the son of the Sapa Inca and his Quitoan wife, Paccha Duchicela, and was therefore based in Ecuador. Since he had been raised in that part of the empire, Atahualpa had the backing of the Ecuadorian people of the Inca Empire, who had always been resistant to the Inca but had put up with their suzerainty after the royal marriage had taken place. After the death of his father, Atahualpa took over the rule of the north. Thus, he did not directly challenge his brother, who was situated in Cusco. In fact, when Huáscar became the new Sapa Inca, Atahualpa sent him a delegation with gifts, honoring and respecting his brother as the new king. However, Huáscar was disappointed at the fact that Atahualpa had not appeared before him in person. He declared Atahualpa to be a traitor, executed his messengers, and declared war on his brother, aiming to seize the northern lands from him. The civil war started, and it would only bring more death and destruction to the Inca realm.

The exact events that transpired during the civil war are unknown since the only sources we have from the time are Spanish accounts, which were assembled according to the narratives of the natives after the civil war had already ended. It is not unlikely that these accounts were deliberately distorted by Pizarro and his men to shape a justifying narrative of their subsequent conquest of the empire by inaccurately depicting one side or the other. In any case, many battles were fought between the two brothers' armies throughout the course of the civil war.

One of the early encounters took place in the north near the town of Tumebamba, which is now the Ecuadorian city of Cuenca. There, Atahualpa was ambushed by Huáscar's forces and actually fell prisoner, but he managed to escape at night with the help of one of Huáscar's maidens when the soldiers were busy celebrating their victory. Fleeing to Quito, where a large army was waiting for him, Atahualpa managed to retaliate, slowly achieving victory in the battles that ensued from 1530 to 1532. The ambush at Tumebamba appears to have been Huáscar's only major triumph of Huáscar in the civil war, while Atahualpa's forces managed to emerge victorious in most of the important encounters.

Although Atahualpa possessed a much more approachable personality than his rival, he was ruthless during the war. Upon encountering the enemy forces, he acted decisively but always offered the men under Huáscar to join his army to avoid bloodshed if he had the opportunity. Still, during one of the encounters where Atahualpa managed to defeat one of Huáscar's more experienced generals, he supposedly tortured and executed the general to demonstrate his superiority. Then, he turned his skull into a cup, which he was still using when the Spanish arrived a couple of years later.

Thanks to the prowess of Atahualpa's soldiers, who deeply respected him and even viewed him as a liberator from the tyrannical rule of Huáscar, the important city of Cajamarca was captured. Atahualpa triumphantly entered the city and decided to stay there, sending his trusted generals to deal with the remainder of Huáscar's forces in the following encounters. Huáscar was routed and captured in a battle in January 1532 near Cusco. The capital was seized by Atahualpa's generals, who proceeded to kill all of the people who still did not support their king.

Massacre at Cajamarca

Around the same time that Huáscar's forces were being crushed at Cusco, Francisco Pizarro's third expedition made its way to the Inca lands from Panama. Pizarro and his men set out from Panama and arrived in Ecuador by sea in 1531, landing first at the island of Puná before regrouping and making their way to Tumbes, which they had visited during the previous expedition. This time, however, they found the place to be almost completely destroyed, with only a few inhabitants living in what once was a prosperous town. The locals explained to the conquistadors that the city had declined due to a combination of factors, including the civil war, attacks from neighboring tribes, and a deadly disease. Surprised, Pizarro decided to lead his men deeper into the native lands, hopeful to finally strike the source of the wealth he had encountered during his previous expeditions. Pizarro founded the first permanent Spanish settlement in northwestern Peru, Piura, and left a small garrison behind before heading into the Inca heart of Peru.

As the Spaniards made their way south, heading toward Cusco, they learned of the brutal civil war that had brought devastation to many areas of the empire. As the local communities and towns were split in their support of one of the warring brothers, Pizarro and his men decided not to declare their allegiance to either one. Instead, they would lie to the locals whenever they encountered them, telling them they were on the same side. The conquistadors approached the city of Cajamarca in the late autumn of 1532. On their way, they tried to remain as neutral as they could to minimize their losses and not cause hostility from the natives, but when they learned that Atahualpa was residing in the city, they decided to change their approach.

Before seeing Atahualpa, who was already in a winning position in the civil war, Pizarro sent a messenger to the future Sapa Inca. The messenger, Hernando de Soto, who would later on become known for his expeditions to the modern-day United States, was told to describe the conquistadors as followers of the "true" God to convince Atahualpa to allow them to enter the city.

Historians today debate whether or not the Inca, who had already had contact with the conquistadors, considered them divine, God-sent creatures by the time they arrived at Cajamarca. It is believed that a notion along these lines existed within the natives, although they had been skeptical about treating the Spaniards as the servants of God.

But since de Soto had come in peace and offered friendship and gifts, Atahualpa had no reason to deny them entry into the city. According to Spanish records, de Soto was able to impress Atahualpa with the horse he had been riding. The Inca had never seen the animal before and was amazed by the Spaniard's excellent horsemanship, making him even more intrigued by what the conquistadors wanted in his realm.

Although Atahualpa expressed his initial concerns about the intent of the conquistadors, referring to reports that men like them had not been friendly toward the natives in the north, he still let them through to Cajamarca. But what happened next remains unclear. The conquistadors entered Cajamarca in November 1532, probably already having discussed their plan of action. Their objective was to seize Atahualpa once they had been let inside the city, as they believed they would not obtain victory otherwise. The two sides agreed to meet in the central plaza of the city the following day, on November 16th.

Pizarro had about 160 men at his disposal, all of them armed to the teeth with swords and wearing armor. Most had guns, while a small part of the conquistadors was on horseback. On the other hand, Atahualpa came to the meeting with at least a couple of thousand men, according to Spanish records. His guards were not armed, and they only carried small tomahawks. The natives were dressed in lavish ceremonial clothes, and Atahualpa sat on a litter, which was decorated in gold.

It was clear the Inca had considered the meeting with the Spanish some sort of a ritual, as he had deliberately ordered his army to stay outside of the city walls, about half a mile from Cajamarca. Maybe he wanted to impress the Spanish by displaying a fraction of his power. In any case, Pizarro and Atahualpa met, for the first time, inside the city in mid-November 1532.

During the meeting, a Spanish friar by the name of Vincente de Valverde approached Atahualpa with an interpreter, carrying a Bible, which he presented to the Inca. He spoke on behalf of the conquistadors, declaring that they had been sent by the true God as his emissaries and that Atahualpa was commanded by God to accept Him. In addition, the friar told the Inca that the conquistadors were also representatives of Spain's King Charles and that the Inca were to recognize their new suzerain.

Atahualpa was not only intrigued but also insulted by the friar's remarks. He tried to ask questions about the god the conquistadors spoke of but became more upset when the interpreter was unable to effectively translate Valverde's answers in detail. Everyone realized the meeting was not going smoothly. The Sapa Inca's dissatisfaction became clear when he threw the Bible the friar had given him to the ground as a sign of disrespect.

Whether it was due to the disrespectful behavior of the Sapa Inca or Pizarro's plan of action, the situation escalated quickly. The conquistadors started attacking the natives who accompanied the emperor, massacring them to get to Atahualpa. The Inca were caught off-guard by this. Although they heavily outnumbered the conquistadors, they were unable to properly fight back because they did not have any weapons. It was a bloody battle, if it can even be called that, and thousands of natives fell to the might of Spanish swords and guns. They were forced to flee the plaza and abandon Atahualpa, who was seized by Pizarro soon after the start of the battle.

Word spread quickly to the professional Inca forces camped outside the city, but they were unable to produce a quick response since their leader was already captured by the enemy. With the Sapa Inca imprisoned, the Inca warriors were hesitant to act on their own. The hospitality of the Inca had been repaid with blood.

Atahualpa was taken captive by Pizarro, and the conquistadors were free to pillage the city of Cajamarca for valuables. The Sapa Inca pleaded for his freedom, offering the conquistadors safety and his support. Nothing seemed to work, and Atahualpa supposedly offered Pizarro enough gold to fill the room where he was being kept, up to the height reached by his arm, in addition to other rooms filled with silver. The Spaniard was impressed by the offer and was curious to see if he could truly afford to fulfill his promise. He gave Atahualpa two months. Atahualpa did fill up the room with gold, an act whose absurdness should not be understated. When roughly converted to contemporary Spanish pesos and then to modern US currency, the amount of gold Atahualpa gathered in just one room comes out to around half a billion US dollars. When we add this to what the conquistadors took from the great Inca cities in the following raids, it is clear that Pizarro's conquest managed to accumulate the most loot out of all of the other expeditions in the New World.

After delivering his promise, Atahualpa demanded to be released. He was kept in prison for several months as Pizarro and the conquistadors consolidated their position in the city and awaited reinforcements, which eventually arrived in early 1533. In addition, they negotiated with the remnants of the rival civil war faction to avoid being targeted by them, saying they had managed to defeat Atahualpa in one day to demonstrate their prowess. Pizarro also made Atahualpa order his men to bring all of the riches from the biggest cities of the empire to Cajamarca, threatening to kill him if they did not comply.

Once he had gathered thousands of pounds worth of gold, much more than what Pizarro's men would have needed or wanted in their lifetimes, the conquistador commander gathered up his forces to discuss what to do with Atahualpa, whom he believed was of little use. After much consideration, the Sapa Inca was put on a public trial, where he was condemned with several different charges, including idolatry, adultery, polygamy, usurpation of the Inca throne, murdering his brother, and other crimes. The trial concluded that Atahualpa's punishment was death.

In late August of 1533, Atahualpa was sentenced to be burned to death, but he was offered the choice to convert to Christianity. He decided to convert since he believed his soul would not go to the afterlife if his body was burned. The emperor was baptized the following day as Francisco Atahualpa, named after his defeater, Francisco Pizarro. He was executed by garroting, an equally brutal practice that saw the victim strangled to death with a special device. Atahualpa's body was first buried in Cajamarca but was probably later transported to Quito, which he had requested to be his final resting place. Still, the conquest of the Inca Empire was not over.

Completing the Conquest

Despite Atahualpa's execution in 1533, the Spanish conquest of the Inca territories would get increasingly complicated, as new actors would emerge with conflicting interests. Among the rivalries that developed after the massacre at Cajamarca was one between Pizarro and his long-time friend, Diego de Almagro, who had reinforced Pizarro with a couple of hundred men after the conquistadors had captured Atahualpa. The main conflict was over which men would take the majority of the booty obtained from the Inca cities. As other conquistadors arrived with their own forces, more and more problems began to arise, leading to an eventual rebellion against Pizarro in 1535.

Almagro consolidated his position after his expeditions to the south in modern-day Chile, after which a full-scale "civil war" broke out. Different Spanish factions tried to assert their authority over the other with the help of local native groups. As for the natives themselves, they had no real opportunities to resist the conquest. They were too afraid to rise up against the Spanish, whose numbers were increasing monthly. By the end of 1535, more *encomiendas* were set up in Peru, and the region was explored much more thoroughly by the conquistadors, which led to even more colonizers arriving by sea, landing at Piura and then making their way to settle the Inca lands independently, complicating the situation.

The period of warfare and chaos persisted in the Inca lands, mostly in what is today Peru, even after the territory was recognized as a separate viceroyalty in 1542. Almagro was imprisoned and killed in 1538, while Pizarro, the architect of the conquest of the Inca, would be murdered by his compatriots in 1541. Even the establishment of the viceroyalty and the arrival of new conquistadors, who came from Spain with royal orders, did not de-escalate the situation.

The state of civil disorder continued largely until the arrival of Francisco de Toledo, who was appointed as the viceroy in 1569. He is considered to be the man who reorganized the viceroyalty and consolidated the position of the Crown, putting an end to the infighting. In fact, to demonstrate that he meant business, Francisco de Toledo proceeded to capture and execute the last supposed Inca heir, Túpac

Amaru, asserting his dominance over the Inca.

Still, despite the problems of finishing the conquest of Peru, the new viceroyalty would become just as prosperous as its neighbor to the north (the Viceroyalty of New Spain). Peru became a center of outward expansion in South America, assuming the role from Gran Colombia. Conquistadors, such as Pedro de Valdivia, campaigned south to the modern-day territories of Chile and Argentina, colonizing the Mapuche people in the 1540s. This campaign largely completed the Spanish conquest of South America, which had started against the Chibcha and Muisca peoples of the north and continued with the destruction of the Inca Empire.

Historians regard the collapse of the Inca Empire as the final large-scale military conquest of the conquistadors. Expeditions continued throughout the 16th century, but they can hardly be called conquests since the people groups that would come to be dominated by the Spanish colonizers were not nearly as advanced as the native societies of Mesoamerica, Mexico, and Peru.

After gaining control of Peru, the next destination for expansion for the Spaniards was to the south, into the territories of modern-day Chile and Argentina, the region known as La Plata. Sebastian Cabot's expedition explored the area in the late 1520s, but the main Spanish settlement of Buenos Aires was soon abandoned since the area was far too remote from the other Spanish colonies of South America. Beginning in the late 1530s, the area was gradually occupied by conquistadors from Peru and Colombia, who founded the cities of Santiago del Estero, Córdoba, and Tucumán. Although some military activities were organized against the Chaco people of La Plata, the southern peoples were assimilated into the Spanish colonies, much like the native inhabitants of the Caribbean islands. They did not want to fight against Spanish weapons, so they chose to reluctantly agree to their new suzerain's rule. The *encomienda* system was also established in South America, but due to the changes the system underwent in the mid-16th century, it was no longer as exploitative as at the beginning of the age of colonization.

Spanish colonization never really kicked off in the Amazon River Basin. This was mainly due to the fact that the Amazon rainforest was very difficult to explore, as it was full of countless natural threats. Few conquistadors dared to enter the Amazon and find out what dwelled in its shadows, afraid they would meet a gruesome end either at the hands of hostile natives, who were known to inhabit the rainforest, or deadly insects and predators of the jungle. The peoples of the Amazon were more primitive anyways because they lived in the jungle, secluded from more prosperous civilizations who inhabited hospitable areas. So, the jungle was largely left unexplored and uncolonized. The Amazon is still considered to be one of the most mysterious places on Earth. Thanks to recent technological developments, more and more parts of the rainforest are slowly being unearthed, and the remnants of the primitive native inhabitants of the Amazon are being discovered.

Chapter Seven – Spanish America

Factors of Spanish Success

Having covered the main Spanish conquests in the Americas throughout the first half of the 16th century, it is now time to look at the colonies themselves. Eventually, the colonies would develop into complex political entities and have special relations with each other and the Spanish Crown back in Europe. Exploring the social, political, and economic circumstances that played a role in the formation of the Spanish colonies is very interesting, but before we get to that, let's once again look at the main factors that helped the conquistadors achieve success when it came to their conquest of the Americas.

The main war efforts that were undertaken by the Spanish in the Americas can roughly be dated from Cortés's expedition in 1519 in Mexico to the 1540s when the conquistadors managed to take control of most of South America. Cortés basically provided his successor conquistadors with the model of a military campaign that could be used to conquer the natives in different parts of the New World.

The main reason behind the obvious successes of the Spaniards when it came to colonization was their technological superiority in warfare. Spanish armies had a long-standing military tradition by the time the conquistadors set their eyes on the Americas, which meant they were more experienced. The newest addition to their arsenal was gunpowder, which had reached Europe for the first time in the 13th century but had come to increasingly dominate the militaries of the continent. By the time Columbus reached the New World, gunpowder weapons had advanced to the point that they were very effective at killing. The natives had never even had access to such developed weaponry. The natives could only answer with bows; they did not even have crossbows, another lethal ranged weapon. They were scared to death by the roars of Spanish guns and the horses, which they regarded as beastly, magnificent creatures.

Cortés's campaign against the Aztecs demonstrated other weaknesses of the natives, like the fact the Spanish could gain a psychological edge over their more primitive opponents. Many native peoples were extremely superstitious and religious, placing a big emphasis on tales and mystical accounts that talked about the arrival of bearded strangers from the east. It is not completely illogical to say that the conquistadors were sometimes viewed as actual deities by the natives. Although this factor is largely exaggerated in Spanish accounts and has become more of a myth in popular culture, it surely played a role in the domination of the superstitious natives.

The underlying objective of most, if not all, conquistadors was to obtain personal wealth from their expeditions into the unknown. As far as they were concerned, the New World offered them the opportunity to become rich beyond belief, at least certainly more than they had been in their previous lives in Spain. They dared to go on dangerous journeys into unexplored territory for personal reasons. A more general, imperialist, and almost evangelical notion of colonization, which emphasized the fact that the colonizers were spreading enlightenment and the word of God to the "primitive" people of the New World, came a bit later.

Yes, the strong Christian tradition played a big role from the very early days of colonization. The Christianization of the natives eventually emerged as a general objective once more reliable links to the New World were organized. But primarily, the conquistadors sought material gains. They knew or at least had a rough idea of the gold that supposedly existed in the New World from others who had already undertaken the journey. And if we take into consideration the fact that the medieval European social structure was rigid, not allowing for social mobility, it is quite easy to understand why many people chose to leave their lives behind in search of new ones in the New World. Plus, the success and subsequent notoriety of Cortés and his crew motivated conquistadors to try their luck in the Americas, hoping that it would bring them eternal glory and fame and elevate them to the status of legends like Cortés himself.

The Encomienda

We have already talked about the *encomienda*, a labor system introduced by the Spanish that helped shape the colonial relationships between the colonizers and the colonized since the discovery of the New World. The main reason behind the establishment of such a system was to stop the natives from competing with the Spaniards. Ultimately, the conquistadors needed some way of asserting their dominance over the natives to help them assimilate the conquered peoples of the Americas into a hierarchical societal structure. The Spanish wanted to grow their settlements and permanently obtain control, which would, in turn, translate into a new reliable channel of income to the mainland that could be used by the Crown to increase its standing in Europe.

Thus, the *encomienda* was just a part of a larger system envisioned by the Spanish Crown to consolidate the gains of the New World. Since we have extensively covered the military affairs between the Spanish and the indigenous people, it is now worth looking at the system that enabled the conquistadors to retain and extend their presence in the newly conquered lands.

The prototype for establishing the *encomienda* system in the Americas was the Reconquista, a long process during which Spanish and Portuguese kingdoms reconquered Iberian lands from the Muslims. When Spanish Christian knights successfully occupied former Muslim lands, the Crown granted them jurisdiction over the people who lived in those lands to control the newly conquered territories more effectively. This decentralization of power through the knights proved successful, as the Iberian kingdoms during the early to middle stages of the Reconquista were far too weak to exercise centralized control over the reconquered lands. The system had helped the Spanish in Europe, and since the circumstances in the newly discovered lands in the Americas were comparable to that of Iberia during the Reconquista, the colonizers thought it would be logical to exercise it in similar ways in the New World.

So, in the New World, the purpose of the *encomienda*, which would traditionally be issued as a formal grant, was to designate native families or whole settlements to the charge of a Spanish colonist, thus making him the *encomendero*. The natives in a specific *encomienda* would pay tribute and work for the *encomendero*, who would enjoy the benefits of the natives' labor. In return for the income, the colonizers "offered" military obligations, meaning they would defend the native subjects in cases of war. Another major thing the *encomenderos* were responsible for was the Christianization of the native people who were entrusted to them through the grant. This was the gist of how the *encomienda* system worked in the Americas, but, of course, the reality was not this simple.

The *encomienda* system was exercised in a highly uncontrolled and exploitative way since the beginning of colonization, especially before Cortés's expedition into the Aztec lands. The first stage of Spanish colonial activity was concentrated on the settlement of the Caribbean West Indies, where the *encomienda* was a logical solution to the labor problem. The Spanish settlers were few, so if they wanted to settle permanently in the New World, they could not rely only on themselves. But the *encomienda* was not always organized, thanks to relations between the colonizers and the colonized. The natives did greet the Spaniards with respect and hospitality in many places, but they would seldom agree to the proposal to work for the newly arrived and strange Europeans. When labor was not provided voluntarily, the conquistadors were more than happy to force them to do it. In turn, this caused a chain reaction. More and more colonizers arrived almost every month in the colonies, increasing the burden that fell on the native people who worked in the *encomiendas*. The Spanish justified the use of force since they regarded the natives as inferior, treating them as they had treated the natives of Africa. Ultimately, early *encomiendas* were so exploitative that it was basically Spanish slavery, although the colonizers themselves would not admit that.

Back in Iberia, the Spanish monarchy's position toward what was essentially slavery was ambiguous, to say the least. Queen Isabella saw the Christianization of the natives as something completely normal and appreciated the fact that the *encomenderos* made sure it happened. However, when confronted with the reality of forced labor, she tended to justify it. In her view, those natives who resisted the colonizers and were hostile toward them should be punished, and the *encomienda* was a great way of guaranteeing that they would show their allegiance to the Spaniards. She explicitly remarked that the natives were not slaves. They could not be bought or sold, and the colonizers treated them humanely. In her opinion, they were "free" people under the jurisdiction of the Spanish Crown. Therefore, just like the other subjects of the Crown, they were to pay tribute to the monarchy in some way, and the *encomienda* was how they could. Through their labor, as exploitative as it might have been, they were responsible citizens of the Spanish Empire.

However, in the West Indies, the natives were very much treated like slaves. They were formally distributed among the *encomenderos*, who placed the natives under their control to do whatever they saw fit, be it agriculture, mining, or some other endeavor. The relocation and redistribution of native labor disrupted the dynamics of native life, which had been intact for generations and had emerged as a societal norm. The natives of the Caribbean once had their lives organized based on different roles, but their peaceful equilibrium was completely destroyed by the colonizers, who did not understand that the natives were dependent on whatever they had been doing before the arrival of the Spanish. Thus, not only were the natives in the *encomienda* overworked, abused, bought, and sold, but the colonizers were also directly responsible for disrupting their societal structures, leading to many cases of widespread famine since fewer natives would be assigned jobs in agriculture. The early *encomienda* was a tragedy.

Regulating the *encomienda* proved to be extremely difficult. The main reason, aside from the lack of initiative from authoritative figures, was the inability to enforce the laws. The first major legislation that sought to transform the nature of the *encomienda* system is known as the Laws of Burgos. It was a code of Spanish-native relations promulgated by King Ferdinand's court in the year 1512, which was still relatively early in the colonization process. The laws were considered to be a response to the humanitarian protests of the missionaries of the Dominican Order, who had been very vocal in criticizing the unchristian nature of the *encomienda* after their travels to the New World.

The Laws of Burgos outlined a few new things. The natives were officially declared not to be slaves, with the legislation stressing the fact that they should not be mistreated since they were regular subjects of the empire. The Christianization of the natives was to become a new priority for the *encomenderos*. And the *encomiendas* were to be limited in size to prevent the emergence of uncontrollable entities. However, the Laws of Burgos were ineffective. The governors in the West Indies who were tasked with the enforcement of the royal laws did not really possess that much authority over the *encomenderos*, who held the real power in the colonies as the richest class. Thus, the legislation did not really achieve its goals.

The following years saw the "golden age" of the *encomienda*, as Cortés's expedition gained more lands to establish new *encomiendas* in the formerly prosperous Aztec territories. Despite King Charles V's initial efforts to abolish the exploitative practice (here again, religious forces were involved to influence the monarch's attitude), Cortés personally refused to obey in his letters to the king. The conquistador basically stated that his crew saw the newly conquered lands as rewards for their services to the Crown; after all, they had colonized and explored the New World in the name of the king. Cortés thus believed that the abolition of the *encomienda* was outright impossible. The Mexican *encomiendas* were also much more productive and efficient in comparison to the ones organized in the less wealthy West Indies, something that reinforced Cortés's argument.

This argument persuaded the king, and the *encomienda* was left alone for a long time, flourishing as the Spanish conquest of the Americas reached its peak. *Encomiendas* were extensively organized in Mesoamerica, although they retained their inhumane attributes. Cortés became a lavish *encomendero* with his possessions in the Valley of Oaxaca, and it is likely that he did not want the system abolished because it guaranteed him great wealth and status.

The *encomendero* class rose to prominence, reaching its peak in the late 1530s. Essentially, they were the feudal lords of the New World, transforming the *encomienda* into a means of control, prestige, and power. Efforts were made to increase their position even more, with the *encomenderos* making the *encomienda* an inheritable possession, something that clashed with the original intent of the royal grants.

What could the Crown do to stop this? The answer is not that much. Effectively enforcing the legislation from Iberia was impossible, and upsetting the *encomenderos* was a guaranteed way to create instability. Nevertheless, King Charles tried to change the system, seeing it as an essential point in exercising royal authority over the expanding colonies. The New Laws, which were passed in 1542, sought to do that.

The New Laws, much like the Laws of Burgos thirty years earlier, stated that an inherently Christian and humane relationship should be maintained between the colonizers and the natives, even if the latter were "primitive heathens." The New Laws prohibited native enslavement, even as a means of punishment. New *encomiendas* were not to be granted anymore, largely due to the fact that almost everything had been colonized by that point. Royal officers, soldiers, and ecclesiastic figures were to step down from the ownership of their *encomiendas* to distinguish between the Crown's servants and private citizens. More regulations were implemented when it came to the collection of tribute and distribution of labor in the *encomiendas*. And most importantly, the *encomienda* was to stop being a hereditary possession.

It is not hard to guess the general reaction the laws caused in the New World upon their promulgation. Yes, by this time, the situation was more stabilized, and governance was more organized by a better administrative structure, but it was not nearly enough to enforce the New Laws to the extent it was intended by the Crown. The *encomendero* class, having grown to a whole new level, opposed it. They even organized protests and riots in many areas like Peru. In some colonies, the governors were simply too "afraid" to try to enforce the new laws, believing it to be too insulting to their subjects. They were unwilling to witness the consequences it might bring. Most importantly, however, the outcry of the *encomenderos* was directed to the fact that the *encomiendas* were to lose their hereditary status, something that was deemed unacceptable. The pressure exerted by the *encomenderos* made King Charles give in again. He repealed the code after a couple of years to the excitement and joy of the colonists.

The *encomienda* system saw many more regulations and changes to it throughout the years, none of which were particularly effective in undermining its dominance as the most powerful socioeconomic system of the New World. Some limitations did make it through, despite the Crown's inconsistent approach. What really contributed to the decline of the *encomienda* was not the legal factors introduced by the monarchy; instead, it was the gradual decline of the native population due to a multitude of factors, most importantly disease.

The *encomienda* system was always dependent on large numbers of natives working for the colonizers. In the beginning, this was easy to maintain, but as the Spaniards became more closely intertwined with the natives, the flaws of the system started to show. The number of natives who died in the Spanish conquests up to the 1540s pales in comparison to the number who fell victim to deadly diseases introduced to the New World by the Europeans. This was especially true for areas that were densely populated, like the big cities in the Aztec and Inca lands. By the early 17th century, these areas were almost completely devoid of native life when compared to the late 15th century, the time of Columbus's expeditions. The exact numbers are not clear, but more than 90 percent of the native population of the New World is thought to have perished in the first one hundred years of the age of colonization.

In turn, this horrific circumstance undermined the power of the *encomenderos*, who had been dependent on the natives for a long time. However, there were fewer and fewer natives to force into the *encomienda*. The native depopulation was a phenomenon that was, to put it simply, uncontrollable at the time. No legislation or enactment could prevent the spread of disease, let alone the lack of advanced medical tools available in the 16th century. In addition to smallpox, measles and typhoid epidemics hit the densely populated native civilizations of the Americas especially hard, decimating them and upsetting the ethnic balance in the region. Europeans contracted syphilis from the natives, but its consequences were nowhere as severe.

Thus, when human resources—the most integral part of the *encomienda*—were slowly depleted, the *encomienda* system itself was prone to decline. The adjustments made by the *encomenderos* were useless since the native depopulation continued at a steady pace before eventually reaching the point when the *encomienda* could no longer be regarded as a sustainable income source. As more and more colonizers flocked into the New World with the intention of gaining wealth, the *encomienda* system declined even more until continuing the practice no longer made sense.

In the later stages of colonization, the power of the *encomenderos* started to decline rapidly, and they were forced to seek financial help from other means, like the Crown. But even the funds provided by the monarchy were insufficient when it came to the *encomiendas'* revival. Eventually, in the 18th century, the system would be finally abolished, but at that time, it no longer held the significant position it had once enjoyed. Through intermarriage and more intensive colonization, the lands of the New World were slowly repopulated, giving rise to new social classes that would primarily be based on a person's race.

Nevertheless, the *encomienda* was a central aspect of the early colonial activities of the Spanish Empire in the Americas. It was a system that proved to bring out the worst qualities of the power-hungry conquistadors, transforming them from brave individuals who sought to obtain glory and wealth in the New World to a selfish bourgeois class that exploited the powerless native populations. The *encomienda* provided the basis for the class distinctions that would emerge in the later periods of Spanish colonization of the Americas, affecting the social outlook of the colonies hundreds of years after its initial implementation. The *encomienda* remains one of the most important institutions of Spanish colonial America.

The Church

Let's now devote some time to talking about the role the Catholic Church played in the Spanish colonization of the Americas. The church was another instrument that radically shaped the Spanish colonies, something that should not come as a surprise based on the general importance of religion in medieval Spain.

In fact, it is not completely untrue to say that Christianity was a formative part of Spain's identity at the time. The kingdom had come into being after a couple of hundred years of struggle between the Catholic rulers of Iberia against the Muslims who controlled most of the peninsula at the dawn of the millennium. Centuries of back-and-forth would eventually end in the Christians' triumph. They had almost completely forced the Muslims out of Iberia by the time Columbus made his first expedition to the New World.

The church was already a well-established institution in Spain by the time colonization kicked off in the late 15th century, and the kingdom also had a tight relationship with the papacy, something that was also very necessary at the time. The experience of converting Muslims and other non-believers during the Reconquista laid the groundwork for Spanish colonizers to transform the religious life of the natives.

Still, even if the Christianization of the natives was the formal justification of the Spanish conquests, we have already seen that, in practice, the rule exercised by the conquistadors in the New World was not at all "Christian." Especially in the earliest stages of colonization, the explorers were motivated by the prospects of gaining wealth and eternal glory. They were more than happy to exploit the natives in their terrible labor systems with little regard for Christianization. In any case, we can see today that the Latin American countries, the majority of which were once former Spanish colonies, are very religious, signaling that the Catholic Church made a long-lasting impact. Thus, the history of the Christianization of the New World and the subsequent emergence of the church as its central institution is very important to examine.

As historians have pointed out, despite the lustful and selfish objectives of many of the early colonizers, it is not fair to say that no one was motivated to spread the word of God. Catholic friars from different religious orders accompanied each expedition, and many of them regarded the missionary activities they undertook in the New World as their purpose. The developments of the late 15th century in religious thought certainly influenced the devout missionaries who embarked on mass conversions of the natives.

With the unification of Spain and the successes in the Reconquista, Catholicism emerged as a central part of Spanish society, and in addition to this sense of a "national religion," there seemed to be an accompanying new Christian purpose, which showed itself in the activities of the missionaries in the Americas. This new role had been influenced by the emergence of humanism in Renaissance Europe, which emphasized learning, scholasticism, and the social and moral high grounds, which were essential to be considered a good Christian. The extensive education of Spanish religious figures in the early 16th century, especially in the Latin, Hebrew, and Greek languages, was useful when the missionaries arrived in the New World. The skills they had gathered during their learning were utilized extensively to get a grasp of the native languages, which was crucial if they wanted to communicate the word of God to the natives.

Another message of Christian humanism, propagated by Erasmus of Rotterdam, one of the most influential figures in the history of medieval Christianity, heavily influenced the Spanish missionary activities in the Americas. This message emphasized the potential degree of greatness and goodness that could be achieved by everyone who lived by the principles of Christianity. Erasmus's writings were taken somewhat literally by the Spanish missionaries, who believed this part of Christian humanism could be directly applied to the pagan peoples of the New World. If, as Erasmus had said, the Europeans had been corrupted and could only achieve greatness by following Christian teachings, why could not the same be applied to the natives? The missionary friars believed the natives could be not only Christianized but also civilized in this regard, shaping their outlook on early evangelism. To the evangelists, the natives were to be shown the truth and purified.

Of course, this was easier said than done, and missionary friars experienced countless problems. The biggest obstacle was the fact that the natives had just been conquered and exploited by the conquistadors, who were the true leaders of colonial activities. Hence, the natives regarded the friars to be just as exploitative as their conquistador compatriots, and in many cases, they were hostile toward them, despite the latter's good intentions. Obviously, the language barrier also posed a big problem to the missionaries, as they found it very difficult to properly communicate their message to the natives when they first arrived.

Furthermore, the makeup of native religions was very complex and profoundly anti-Christian. Native religions were mostly polytheistic and based upon rituals and ceremonies, which sometimes involved anti-Christian ideas like human sacrifice, cannibalism, or the attribution of divinity to material objects. Many missionaries adopted a very negative outlook toward the natives, regarding them as unconvertible heathens whose pagan ways could never be replaced by virtuous Christian lifestyles. Even when there were some similarities with Christianity, such as the occasional use of the symbol of the cross in some native religions or the existence of creation myths, these made the friars' jobs all the more difficult. The missionaries dismissed the native religions as wholly pagan and realized they had to Christianize all aspects of their lives.

To counter these problems, the friars had to come up with strategies that distinguished them from the more violent conquistadors, who had come to be associated with exploitation in the eyes of the natives. One of the practices adopted by the early missionaries was to divide into groups of two or three and go around the native communities unarmed and barefoot to preach. At first, they communicated with the help of local interpreters but soon devoted a lot of time to learning native languages, such as Nahuatl, to spread the word of God more effectively. In order to convince many people to convert at once, the friars also focused on converting the leaders of the native communities since they realized the people would follow their leader even when it came to religious beliefs.

Gradually, the missionaries began to get rid of native rituals, temples, idols, and other things that were deemed devilish and pagan and began to replace them with Christian imagery. Churches were commonly built on top of old temples, symbolizing the fact that the native religion was being replaced by a new one. The natives who voluntarily converted were then used by the missionaries, who assigned them jobs outside of the *encomienda*, such as helping them to construct churches and convents. They treated the converted natives with respect and slowly introduced sacraments other than baptism to highlight their importance in a developing Christian community. More and more natives joined in, resulting in a steady rate of conversions in the first few decades of colonization.

Spain, as well as the papacy, started to soon recognize the job being done by the missionary groups. Things took a turn in Europe during the 16th century when the Protestant Reformation divided Europe into two. Spain, as one of the most fervent defenders of the traditional Catholic faith, emerged as the leader of the Catholic Counter-Reformation to the more German-based Protestantism. In short, as the role of Catholicism was amplified in continental Europe, the missionaries felt the need to increase their evangelical activities in the New World. Protestant missionary activity started to take off in the 17th century, with waves of Protestants arriving in North America, settling in the area of New England and spreading their distinct vision of Christianity there.

This, in turn, resulted in a highly polarized religious landscape in the Americas. As time went on, the Spanish colonies of the New World retained Catholicism as their religion, while the English colonies in North America became increasingly Protestant, choosing one of the many different denominations this new form of Christianity offered. This sort of division between the different areas of the Americas persists to this day.

Despite the failures the church faced in the early stages of colonization, it would eventually emerge as the most hailed institution in the Spanish colonies. Christianity was a vital part of medieval Spanish culture, and due to the freedom available to the colonizers when it came to spreading their religion, they could exclude the other religions of the world in favor of Catholicism, making it essentially the only available version for the natives. Intermarriage and the arrival of more colonizers in the 16th century contributed to the church becoming the most prominent institution of Spanish colonial America.

Christian religious art and architecture of the colonized territories, which flourished beginning in the late 16th century, became a staple of the new culture. Spanish America constructed monumental churches and cathedrals that were in line with other Catholic buildings in Europe, something that again highlights the importance of Catholicism in the Americas. The architectural style of these cathedrals is very similar to traditional Spanish religious architecture in Europe. This was in part due to the fact that building plans would usually be sent directly from Spain or Rome. Still, colonial religious architecture managed to develop its own unique qualities.

The paradoxical nature of the violent, exploitative conquests of the conquistadors and the more humane efforts of missionary friars to Christianize the natives is evident. These two approaches to colonization would eventually clash many times. The religious establishment would emerge as one of the main opponents of the *encomienda* system, causing its eventual decline and making the church the main institution in Spanish America. Although the church would ultimately gain too much power, becoming economically independent and dabbling in power politics in later centuries, its importance in forming today's Latin American society should not be understated. The Catholic Church was eventually seen as a pillar of stability for the people of Spanish America, and as the colonies expanded, so did the Catholic Church's influence.

Conclusion

The rediscovery of the Americas by Christopher Columbus turned the world upside-down, resulting in a series of developments that shaped history. The Age of Exploration, which was ushered in by Columbus's expeditions and the journeys of countless other Spanish and Portuguese explorers, provided new frontiers, challenges, and goals to the brave Europeans who wished to try their luck and venture out into the unknown. The result was colonization, a phenomenon that is sometimes too overwhelming for casual readers to delve deep into because it includes so many different aspects, one of which is conquest. In the eyes of many, conquest was an inevitable part of colonization, owing in part to the general design of the medieval world, which had been forged due to two main things: endless warfare and the influence of religion.

Thus began the Spanish conquest of the New World, although historians state what we call the period of "conquest" started in the year 1519 when Hernán Cortés led his crew on a daring expedition into the lands of the Aztec Empire in modern-day Mexico. Cortés's expedition revolutionized colonization, presenting the Spaniards with new avenues and a tested method for dominating the natives. Before Cortés, Spanish colonial endeavors were done on a relatively smaller scale, partially because the Caribbean islands did not house advanced forms of civilizations like the more developed places in continental America. The early colonizers found it very easy to gain a permanent foothold in the Caribbean islands, forcing the natives into their *encomiendas* relatively easily.

The Spanish conquest of the Americas (in the sense of a large-scale conflict between the conquistadors and the natives) came to an end in the 16th century, although hostilities between the two did not stop for a long time. The Spanish conquest can be divided into three main parts: the takeover of the Aztecs by Cortés; the domination of Maya territories in the Yucatán by Alvarado, Montejo, and others; and the takeover of the Inca Empire by Pizarro. All three endeavors were ultimately successes for the Spaniards and ended in destruction for the natives. The three greatest civilizations of the Americas—the Aztec, the Maya, and the Inca—were dominated one by one by the conquistadors, who were relentless in their approach and blinded by the search for wealth and glory. The Spaniards never backed down, thinking that destiny had awarded them with whatever awaited in the unknown, and they were not hesitant to use every possible means to get to it.

Colonization and conquest were extremely tragic for the natives, most of whom perished not in combat but because they contracted deadly European diseases. The majority of native populations were decimated, with estimates ranging up to 95 percent of all native societies in the Americas. Those who survived were slowly assimilated into the new Spanish society, but it was extremely difficult for them to continue living their lives as they had before the arrival of the conquistadors.

Nevertheless, through sheer will and determination, native ethnic groups managed to retain their diverse cultures, surviving centuries of oppression. These people showed incredible adaptability to the changing turbulent times they were confronted with beginning in the late 15th century.

The Spanish conquest of the Americas is a story of violence, greed, and inhumanity. It is a narrative of how just a few thousand people, coming from thousands of miles away, managed to completely dominate and alter the lives of millions who had prospered in their own civilizations prior to contact. It is an account of a typical war-hungry medieval mindset in its worst possible manifestation. The conquistadors managed to conquer the natives relatively easily and exercised their power over them for hundreds of years. The new society that was established due to colonization was wholly different from the one before it, and in time, it would diverge from the Spanish Empire after a series of revolutions.

Here's another book by Enthralling History that you might like

Free limited time bonus

Stop for a moment. We have a free bonus set up for you. The problem is this: we forget 90% of everything that we read after 7 days. Crazy fact, right? Here's the solution: we've created a printable, 1-page pdf summary for this book that you're reading now. All you have to do to get your free pdf summary is to go to the following website:

https://livetolearn.lpages.co/enthrallinghistory/

Once you do, it will be intuitive. Enjoy, and thank you!

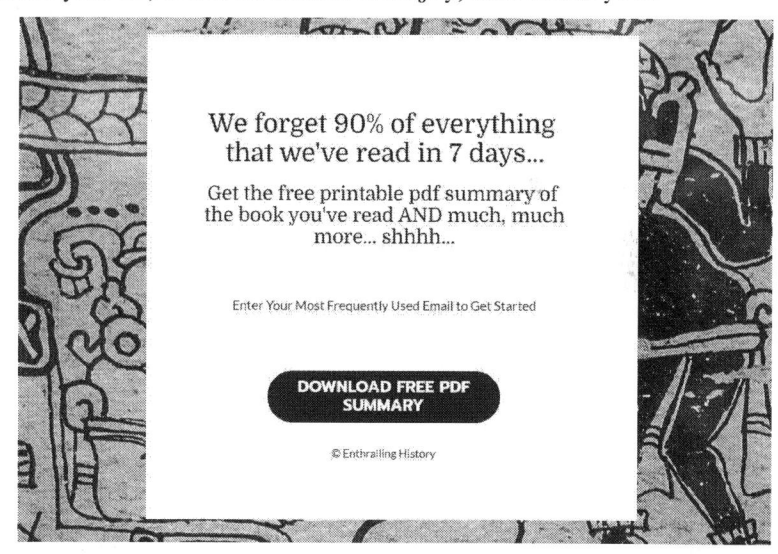

Sources

Brinkerhoff, T. J. (2016). "Reexamining the Lore of the 'Archetypal Conquistador': Hernán Cortés and the Spanish Conquest of the Aztec Empire, 1519-1521." *The History Teacher, 49*(2), 169-187. http://www.jstor.org/stable/24810472

Crosby, A. W. (1967). "Conquistador y Pestilencia: The First New World Pandemic and the Fall of the Great Indian Empires." *The Hispanic American Historical Review, 47*(3), 321-337. https://doi.org/10.2307/2511023

Díaz del Castillo, Bernal & Carrasco, Davíd. (2008). *The History of the Conquest of New Spain*. University of New Mexico Press. Retrieved February 28, 2023

Drennan, R. D. (1995). "Chiefdoms in Northern South America." *Journal of World Prehistory, 9*(3), 301-340. http://www.jstor.org/stable/25801080

Gibson, C. (1967). *Spain in America* ([1st ed.], Ser. The New American Nation Series). Harper & Row.

King, H. (2002). "Gold in Ancient America." *The Metropolitan Museum of Art Bulletin, 59*(4), 5-55. https://doi.org/10.2307/3269153

Michigan Publishing (University of Michigan). (2022). *(Post-)colonial Archipelagos: Comparing the Legacies of Spanish Colonialism in Cuba, Puerto Rico, and the Philippines*. (Burchardt Hans-Jürgen & J. Leinius, Eds.). University of Michigan Press. https://doi.org/10.3998/mpub.11747103

Rowe, J. H. (2006). "The Inca Civil War and the Establishment of Spanish Power in Peru." *Ñawpa Pacha: Journal of Andean Archaeology, 28*, 1-9. http://www.jstor.org/stable/27977824

Todorov, T. (1999). *The Conquest of America: The Question of the Other*. (R. Howard, Trans.). University of Oklahoma Press.

Printed in Great Britain
by Amazon